"Our time demands intentional and focused leadership for transformative change. Efforts to address the social determinants of health are more effective and sustainable when we go beyond service creation or coordination as the main goals for impact. We must also, and perhaps primarily, address policy and systems change. This must be done by intentionally considering the intersection and interdependence between our policies and practices in areas like humane housing, meaningful jobs, equitable education, social and cultural connectedness, thriving and nourishing natural ecosystems, and more. Clinical strategies alone won't lead to healthier outcomes. It is critically important to address the root causes of health problems and eliminate health inequities. Ostrowsky and Davis understand this intrinsically, morally, and practically. Their leadership at RWJBarnabas Health reflects a commitment to creating the pathways for a better tomorrow where all of our neighbors can thrive. We all might take heed and learn from the efforts, examples, and knowledge they share in this comprehensive book. When we embrace, share, and adopt these kinds of strategies, we can help to co-create a living legacy for generations to come."

—Brian Rahmer
VP, Health & Housing, Enterprise Community Partners

"This is an important read at a critical moment in time. If ever there was a time to build a framework—from the ground up in our communities—that systemically addresses the social determinants of health, that time is now. Through partnerships with social and racial justice organizations like mine, RWJBarnabas Health is doing just that by making deep investments in empowering healthy, equitable, and vibrant communities. New Jersey will be better because of these investments."

—Ryan Haygood
President and CEO, New Jersey Institute for Social Justice

"Ostrowsky and Davis have produced a movingly compelling account of how major health care organizations can positively impact their home communities. Their heartfelt and substantively detailed account of RWJBarnabas Health's on-the-ground, collaborative work in Newark, NJ, not only serves as a cutting-edge guidebook for tackling the social determinants of health headon but one that generalizes to the role that all anchor institutions can play in effecting community well-being, prosperity, and opportunity. If only we had more such courageous leaders and organizational change agents!"

—Nancy Cantor
Chancellor, Rutgers University-Newark

"Changing Missions, Changing Lives answers the questions, 'Should health care institutions invest in their communities?' and 'Can community leaders help shape that work?' with a resounding 'Yes!' and 'Yes!' Ostrowsky and Davis detail the challenges and opportunities that anchor institutions like RWJBarnabas Health face in this work, as they blaze a trail for other anchor institutions and public leaders to follow when addressing social determinants of health. Their commitment, passion, and dedication is evident. We are grateful that they are moving the needle and bringing together communities, health care institutions, practitioners, and policy makers to improve the quality of life for all of our residents."

—Staci Berger
President and CEO, Housing and
Community Development Network of New Jersey

BARRY H. OSTROWSKY
MICHELLENE DAVIS, ESQ.

CHANGING MISSIONS, CHANGING LIVES

BARRY H. OSTROWSKY
MICHELLENE DAVIS, ESQ.

CHANGING MISSIONS, CHANGING LIVES

How a **Change Agent**
Can **Turn the Ship**
and **Create Impact**

ForbesBooks

Published by ForbesBooks, Charleston, South Carolina.
Member of Advantage Media Group.

ForbesBooks is a registered trademark, and the ForbesBooks colophon is a trademark of Forbes Media, LLC.

Printed in the United States of America.

10 9 8 7 6 5 4 3 2 1

ISBN: 978-1-94663-346-0
LCCN: 2020908846

Cover design by George Stevens.
Layout design by Mary Hamilton.

This publication is designed to provide accurate and authoritative information in regard to the subject matter covered. It is sold with the understanding that the publisher is not engaged in rendering legal, accounting, or other professional services. If legal advice or other expert assistance is required, the services of a competent professional person should be sought.

Advantage Media Group is proud to be a part of the Tree Neutral® program. Tree Neutral offsets the number of trees consumed in the production and printing of this book by taking proactive steps such as planting trees in direct proportion to the number of trees used to print books. To learn more about Tree Neutral, please visit **www. treeneutral.com.**

TreeNeutral

Since 1917, the Forbes mission has remained constant. Global Champions of Entrepreneurial Capitalism. ForbesBooks exists to further that aim by bringing the Stories, Passion, and Knowledge of top thought leaders to the forefront. ForbesBooks brings you The Best in Business. To be considered for publication, please visit **www.forbesbooks.com.**

We dedicate this to those in our communities who have gone before and those who are yet to come. We want to create a world that is devoid of the systems and structures that prevent you from being your healthiest selves.

CONTENTS

Introduction

BARRY H. OSTROWSKY, PRESIDENT AND CEO

"Why would a healthcare organization involve itself in a social change effort?"

That's the question I hear most often when I talk about the work we're doing in our communities. My enthusiasm for and commitment to this effort, and to making our institutions into true anchor institutions in their respective communities, stems from the fact that I've always seen the business we are in as a social service business. Our major product line has historically been conventional clinical services, but that's just a piece of what I've understood to be our true mission. Even as an undergraduate studying urban planning, I felt that those in healthcare should have a greater role in their respective communities, beyond the conventional clinical platform that we've developed.

In a way, that attitude is in my DNA: certainly, I got my sense of the individual's responsibility to the community from my father through hearing him talk about his values and seeing them in action. Our family owned a paint store that supplied both retail customers and painting contractors, and my father was one of the first in our area to offer credit to minority painters. There came a point at which some of the builders putting up big buildings were required to use a percentage of minority contractors on their construction projects. A building was going up in our area, and one of our minority customers who had a small residential painting business came to see my dad. He said, "I have a chance to get this big painting job—but I don't know how to go about submitting a bid."

I happened to be working in the store that day, and my father took me along with the painter to look at the site. After we walked around it, we came back to the store, and Dad figured out what the bid ought to look like. The painter submitted that bid and got the job—and that success gave him the opportunity to transform his small residential painting business into a certifiable commercial painting business. That experience showed me there are things that we as individuals can do to help provide greater equity to those folks who deserve the opportunity but typically don't get it. Incredibly, that same building is the one in which we now have our corporate headquarters, decades later.

When you have a family business like the one we had, it tends to dominate dinner table conversation. Our customer base was quite diverse, ranging from the very wealthy to the working class. My dad made it clear to us that everyone was to be treated with the same care and courtesy, regardless of who they were or how they looked. That was drilled into my siblings and me from early childhood, and it's an attitude we've all carried with us throughout our lives. What I learned from my father, combined with what I learned in college about approaches to improving our urban areas, dovetailed with my work in healthcare management, where I was given the opportunity to expand the mission from conventional clinical care to the health of our community.

I saw the potential to enthusiastically embrace this kind of social determinant work when I was a practicing lawyer representing healthcare clients. When I took up the reins as a healthcare administrator, our organization was operating successfully and accumulating resources, but I had begun to do my own research about what impact we were making in our communities, particularly vulnerable communities. The information I was gathering certainly suggested that while what we were doing was helpful, it only had a minor effect on the community's health. And while about 10 percent of a community's health is based on genetics, and perhaps 20 percent on what we do as clinicians, the other 70 percent is about social determinants. Couldn't we—shouldn't we—be making a more meaningful and consequential contribution?

With this in mind, I asked Michellene to come in one day and said, "We currently have what's effectively a five-pillar strategy. I want to create a sixth pillar for the organization." I laid out what I had concluded through my less-than-fully-academic research; within our service area, which covers around five million people in our state, we had a number of vulnerable communities in which we had big institutions. We needed to develop a piece of our strategy that addressed that 70 percent impact on the health of the community. I wanted to take that idea to our board and convince them to formally change the mission of the organization from healthcare to health, because while we were certainly providing healthcare, we weren't doing all we could to ensure healthy communities.

Michellene did a great job of building the case for that effort—

gathering the data, doing the study, evaluating our vulnerable communities from a number of perspectives—culminating in a presentation we jointly made to the board of trustees about nine months after our initial meeting in which we explained, "This is what we think our mission ought to be—and here is how we would execute it." We made it clear that this effort was not going to enhance the bottom line of the organization. The dividend would be that future generations would not be relegated to unhappy, unhealthy lives, because we'd make our communities better places to live. Our board enthusiastically embraced it and encouraged us to go forward.

Over the five or so years since then, we've been building the internal infrastructure to execute on that plan, and I'm happy to report that the programs we've introduced have gained traction and gotten good results. It's a work in progress, but the progress is real and quantifiable. If it were up to us, we'd eradicate poverty, but that's not possible. Even so, we can and have stepped beyond the boundaries of what healthcare systems typically do, and if we can help one person at a time, ten people at a time, or one hundred people at a time, that is progress in the right direction.

If you're in the healthcare field, either in or leading a healthcare system, the first thing you have to do is acknowledge that no matter how terrific the clinical services you offer are, those alone won't make the community healthier. Typically, we in healthcare are great believers in what we do, and rightfully so—but the limitations of our impact on the community is also something we have to concede. Once you acknowledge that making a real difference means you have to supplement clinical programs with appropriately developed social programs around these social determinants, then you're on your way.

I know this because as president and chief executive officer of the largest academic medical center system in the state of New

Jersey in a vastly changing industry, I realize that our institutional commitment to going beyond the traditional nonprofit hospital system community benefit makes us an institutional change agent at RWJBarnabas Health. This book chronicles our experience in implementing a massive mission shift in my organization of an affiliated forty-four thousand employees, including nine thousand doctors, an effort more like turning an ocean liner than a rowboat. But turn it we have, going outside of our hospital walls and reaching into the communities, especially out to the populations that face the most challenges, to more fully embrace our anchor institution mission: to step up, lean in, and adopt a true commitment to social impact and community investment.

For me, it's more than a mission; it's personal. I look back at my formative years growing up in Newark with a sense of pride but also with a sense of calling. I fondly recall spending time in my grandparents' house there, as I do my own on Shepard Avenue in the city's South Ward. I had no idea then, attending Maple Avenue School and taking library classes in the same neighborhood, that I would later lead an organization that owned and operated the hospital in which I was born. Having acquired an undergraduate degree in urban planning before going on to law school, I never envisioned myself running a system of hospitals. Yet, under our new mission, my background came full circle as we now find ourselves in discussions and partnerships with community development agencies and housing developers and nontraditional healthcare partner organizations around how we can create healthy homes and healthy families and reinvigorate retail corridors in regions which the renaissance of economic redevelopment has not yet reached.

One of the frustrations, of course, is that progress doesn't happen overnight. You have to be patient. When you build a clinical program, you can recruit a couple of clinicians who come with great reputations and begin to start doing whatever it is that they do, and you can see the results quickly. If you're going to start teaching folks about better nutrition and lifestyle choices, those efforts may show immediate positive returns for the individual but take a lot longer to pay off in measurable ways—and for the most part, no one's reimbursing you for these social programs. The fact is, this work requires an allocation of resources for which the ROI isn't something you'll see on the operating statement. But the returns are no less real or meaningful for us, having redefined our position as an anchor institution in our communities. It's our hope that this book can serve as a kind of map for change agents who want to turn their ships in the same direction.

MICHELLENE DAVIS, ESQ., EXECUTIVE VICE PRESIDENT AND CHIEF CORPORATE AFFAIRS OFFICER

What does it take to change the world, or at least the piece of it you're standing on?

Over the past twenty years, we've seen a paradigmatic shift in the view of corporate engagement in social change as more corporations look beyond their core business to find ways to engage with consumers and stakeholders as change agents, whether it's to promote economic development in historically underserved communities, to source fair trade products, or to promote human rights and social justice. We find ourselves at an interesting point in history, one at which more individuals and corporations are stepping up to say, "Asking the questions isn't enough: we need to be part of the answer." Organizations in all fields and across varied industries are seeing that consumers have an expectation that businesses need to engage with challenges presented in their communities. Consumers and communities have heightened expectations that businesses will lean in to fill gaps in societal needs that government and independent individual efforts either cannot or have not addressed.

It's no longer enough to do well; we must also do good. Why? First, because it's the right and responsible thing to do—and also because it helps us build bridges to our patients, communities, and stakeholders, bridges that strengthen both the communities in which we operate and our own organizations.

Increasingly these efforts toward expanded, outward-facing missions are being spearheaded and led from within the organizations themselves: *intrapreneurial* rather than entrepreneurial. We may not know definitively who anoints people with leadership, but typically those who have changed history have emerged from wherever they may have found themselves, despite title or level of institutional authority. That's how change happens, and in our experience, those who are either stepping up as social innovation entrepreneurs or social innovation intrapreneurs within corporations are more numerous and poised to effectuate institutional and social impact than ever before. The question consumers and engaged stakeholders want us to ask is, "How can my corporation continue to perform well while also achieving long-term sustainable positive social good in the communities in which we are located?" The Edelman Trust Barometer points to this.

The 2016 Edelman Trust Barometer, a global survey of consumer attitudes, found that 80 percent of consumers and other stakeholders expect businesses to focus on solid financial returns and to "play a role in addressing societal issues" such as "education, health care and income inequality."[1] In the United States, "87 percent of the general population" believe that a "business can both make a profit and improve economic and social conditions of the community in which it operates."

When it comes to the healthcare industry, the Edelman Trust Barometer report noted several key takeaways regarding the general public's expectations of healthcare companies:

- Eighty-seven percent of the general population believes that healthcare companies have a larger obligation to address social issues while they run their business and generate profit.

- Only 51 percent of people globally trust healthcare CEOs, and only 41 percent of employees of healthcare companies say their own CEO is engaged in societal issues.

- Knowing the deep commitment many healthcare companies have to societal issues, turning up the volume on these initiatives, and ensuring CEOs are rightfully engaged with them should advance [consumer] trust.

---

1   Edelman, "2016 Edelman Trust Barometer," accessed Sep. 6, 2019, https://www. edelman.com/research/2016-edelman-trust-barometer.

Many within the corporate social responsibility space may have asked some form of "What does it take to change the world?" for a long time. What is different now is that we're taking this into the social innovation sphere, where the challenge is to approach an age-old societal issue in a new way with the aim of creating long-term, sustainable change, not necessarily for this lifetime but for the next generation. How do we as corporate entities justify expenditures that may not generate a traditional return on investment until a generation from now and that we may not necessarily be here to witness? How are we measuring outcomes versus outputs? What does that require us to do differently in order to effectuate the change to which we are called?

In embracing this challenge, RWJBarnabas Health has come to realize several things. Chief among them is that organizational leadership must be mission-driven, because nothing else will see you through the challenges of institutional operational culture change if you're not absolutely crystal clear about your "why." Organizational leadership will need to possess mastery of the skill of persuasion. Obtaining buy-in from those whose support your change effort is essential and requires diplomacy on leadership's part. This work cannot merely be mandated; operationalizing the work requires everyone's cooperation, including those who are not invested and who often do not understand why such change is necessary but whose goodwill at minimum is needed to push the new direction forward. And it takes resilience—a thick skin—because there will always be those who dig in to resist change.

We recently celebrated 119 years at our hospital in Newark, Newark Beth Israel Medical Center/Children's Hospital of New Jersey—yet we still have an appalling black infant mortality rate in that city, worse than three third-world countries in one of the wealthiest states in the country. There's something wrong here. How do you have outcomes that are worse than third-world countries in a city of roughly only three hundred thousand people, which once had five hospitals and currently has three? We had to ask ourselves, What could we do to change that? Clearly, merely having accessible hospitals in close proximity wasn't the answer.

An overarching problem of many large-scale organizations is that while we were *in* the community, we weren't necessarily *of* the community. Like most hospital systems, the vast majority of employees live all over the state. Many of our clinical and administrative staff commute from the suburbs to work at hospitals located in the state's urban cores. Like many other systems of our size needing to operate at economies of scale, our suppliers and providers came from outside the community—often, due to group purchasing organization agreements, from halfway across the country. We didn't hire local, we didn't buy local, so outside of the quality clinical care being practiced, we weren't contributing as much economic stimulus as a solid corporate citizen could to the community around us. But so many of the problems we were seeing in the patient population we serve were direct results of the concentrated poverty that decades-old systemic and structural events had either helped create or contributed to, among them lack of access to healthy and nutritious food, a high unemployment rate, inequity in how large-scale corporations viewed the marketable skill level of community members, and the presence of violence. How could we help and what form should that help take, based upon the most significant needs of the communities in which each of our facilities sit? That is why, at our hospital in Newark, which sits in a food desert, we chose first to address food insecurity, while at our hospital in Somerset, where affordable housing is scarce, we are investing in transitional housing.

And our institution isn't the only one driven to this space: we are happy to be a cofounder and continuing design team member of a learning collaborative of like-minded institutions called the Healthcare Anchor Network (HAN), now forty hospital systems and growing, dedicated to building more inclusive and sustainable local economies. The HAN helps to equip this growing body of anchor-driven institutions by creating a safe space learning collaborative and providing the tools, strategies, case studies, and other practical resources needed to advance an institution's anchor mission, making certain that we are as excited about and equipped to hire from our own backyard as we are about recruiting the next top doc from UCLA.

The work we have undertaken is led by the policy arm of the institution through an equity lens and proceeds by applying the design method through a collective impact approach. Applying the design method helps us to research, plan, launch, tweak, and relaunch along the way rather than to apply the typical plan, plan, plan, plan launch system traditionally utilized in risk-averse corporate and hospital settings. Our implementation of the work provides an opportunity to prototype what social change would look like in a framework of equality, equity, and access.

It had always been our mission to deliver high-quality clinical care to everyone who walked through our doors, with a desire to ensure safety and a culturally competent positive patient experience. The way in which our anchor mission has changed us is that we are now also utilizing our place-based presence to effectuate change in the communities we serve. That means the way in which we hire looks different; the way in which we purchase goods and services looks different; and the way in which we invest in our surrounding communities looks different.

For example, our local hire strategy as applied in our prototype city took the form of our system aligning with the mayor of Newark, New Jersey, local policy partners, universities, and corporations to create Newark2020. Newark2020 is a citywide effort to help close the unemployment gap between the city of Newark and the state of New Jersey by the year 2020, which required the hiring of two thousand twenty Newark residents. Government alone can't do that. The unemployed residents of the city can't do that. The ones who can truly help to move that needle are the large-scale corporations who are here but who have historically not opened our doors, procured from the midsize and small businesses within the community, or intentionally hired locally. We're changing that, and we're seeing powerful, real-world results. We've made new friends and alliances, and we're changing lives in our piece of the world. More, we are developing trust within and among our communities in the old-fashioned way— we're earning it.

You can too.

This book is for you, social change agents, forward-thinking institutions, and disruptors, no matter who you are or where you work. Yes, we are talking to the C-suite occupants, the CEOs, and those in organizational leadership. But the truth is it's for any of you who find yourselves called to leadership, no matter what your title, career level, or industry may be. Your organization can make a difference—and we're here to share the insights, successes and failures, and strategies our organization has adopted through its ongoing process. Turning a big ship requires both a well-charted course and the patience to wait for results. It's going to take a long while before you can see the change in direction, because unlike a canoe, a big ship cannot be turned on a dime. It requires not only socializing your particular mandate but also operationalizing it. Those are two different but equally important elements of taking on an anchor mission in order to create true social impact and deep community investment. And, as with any great mission, none of this can be done alone: each member of the vast RWJBarnabas Health crew of employees has contributed.

At the time of this writing, we're more than twenty-four months into it—and yes, the ship is slowly turning. We hope to inspire you, too, to take the helm, chart the course, and change the world.

CHAPTER ONE

Identifying the Challenge

The challenges in addressing the social determinants of health are multifold. At RWJBarnabas Health (RWJBH), we were faced with a diverse population as well as deeply entrenched attitudes and practices that were not atypical of a large healthcare system. Mirroring the nation, systemic issues that stem from differences in race, ethnicity, class, education, and gender, paired with the biases (conscious and unconscious) that result, are pervasive throughout the state and the RWJBH region, thus offering another challenge. As a result, policies both governmental and institutional mimic the biases of the state's residents. These are challenges that stood, and continue to stand, between us and the creation of a healthier New Jersey.

New Jersey is home to nearly nine million people, and five million reside within the seven-county RWJBH region. When your catchment area is that sizable, you treat the whole spectrum of residents, from the Jersey Shore communities to the central hub of the state in New Brunswick to the highly diverse Jersey City, where 54.5 percent of the population speak languages other than English (more than twice the national average of 21.5 percent[2]), to the seemingly monolithic ethnic community in Newark, New Jersey, where nearly 50 percent are Black or of African descent and which boasts a rich diversity of Caribbean and South and Central Americans yet lacks socioeconomic diversity.[3] Reflective of the state rate, nearly 40 percent of individuals who reside in the region are ALICE (asset limited, income constrained, employed) and struggle to afford food, heat, prescriptions, adequate housing, or sufficient medical care.[4] As a result, they have poorer health outcomes.

"Your zip code is a greater determinant of your lifespan than your genetic code."

—Dr. Tony Iton, social justice advocate, SVP
Building Health Communities

While New Jersey is one of the wealthiest states in the nation, with a median household income of $76,126, the state has pockets of tremendous need as well as communities of great affluence.

---

2   "Jersey City, NJ," Data USA, accessed Jan. 6, 2020, https://datausa.io/profile/geo/jersey-city-nj/#demographics.

3   "Newark, NJ," Data USA, accessed Jan. 6, 2020, https://datausa.io/profile/geo/newark-nj/#demographics.

4   "A Study of Financial Hardship in New Jersey," United Way, accessed Sep. 6, 2019, http://www.unitedwaynnj.org/ourwork/alice_nj.php.

According to Bloomberg News, New Jersey boasts eighteen of the wealthiest places to live, more than any other state in the nation, yet nearly nine hundred twenty thousand New Jerseyans go to bed hungry every night and 1.9 million struggle with overcrowding, high housing costs, or lack of a kitchen or plumbing.[5] An inspection of the RWJBH region depicts similar wealth gaps. For example, Millburn, New Jersey, has a household income of $202,862,[6] nearly three times the state rate and almost six times that of Newark a mere thirteen miles away, where household income is $34,826.[7] Similarly, the average life expectancy for a Newark resident is sixty-eight years old, fourteen years less than the average life expectancy of their neighbors in Livingston.

Like other large-scale organizations, RWJBH suffered from "this is the way it has always been done" syndrome, and in a healthcare setting, we naturally look at problems through the clinical lens; as a healthcare system, the institutional attitude to the challenges in our communities was that improving the standard of care would somehow solve all the problems affecting health outcomes. The thinking has long been that if you recruited a great new head cardiologist or purchased the newest equipment, surely that would impact

---

5   Number of households in NJ, 3,194,519 (http://www.unitedwaynnj.org/
     documents/18UWALICE_NJ_Report_Overview.1.16.19.pdf), multiplied by the 23
     percent that struggle (http://www.countyhealthrankings.org/sites/default/files/
     state/downloads/CHR2019_NJ.pdf) [updated to represent 2019 stats—was 23%]
     = 702,794 households in NJ that struggle, multiplied by 2.74 (avg. NJ household
     size)(https://www.census.gov/quickfacts/nj) = 1,925,656 people.

6   Shelly Heigan and Wei Lu, "These Are the Wealthiest Towns in the US,"
     Bloomberg, accessed Jan. 6, 2020, https://www.bloomberg.com/news/
     articles/2019-02-13/silicon-valley-suburb-snags-richest-spot-in-u-s-for-third-year.

7   "QuickFacts: Newark city, New Jersey; Lakewood CDP, New Jersey; Short Hills
     CDP, New Jersey," Us Census Bureau, accessed Jan. 6, 2020, https://www.census.
     gov/quickfacts/fact/table/newarkcitynewjersey,lakewoodcdpnewjersey,shorthills
     cdpnewjersey/PST045218.

cardiac mortality rates—but while talented clinicians certainly positively impacted clinical quality and care, keeping such a narrow focus did not. Clearly, it was time for the perspective of healthcare delivery systems to change.

The lens through which we must begin to view the health of the community is one that reflects an understanding that the areas in which vulnerable populations present in the greatest concentration have many factors that impact their health: lack of access to healthy food, for instance, or lack of reliable and affordable transportation, or equitable access to living-wage jobs. Too often in situations like these, we blame the victim. It's easy to dismiss a patient who is struggling to make ends meet while also having to navigate a complex health delivery system as merely "medically noncompliant." But this label is a lazy one for an institution, because it assumes that people are choosing not to be healthy, when the truth of the matter is that they struggle just to stay afloat. Certainly, that is the case in municipalities with vulnerable populations throughout the country, such as Newark.

Conversely, vulnerable populations often have deeply entrenched attitudes of their own about healthcare. They often mistrust the establishment, and healthcare has to find creative ways to regain trust and become part of the fabric of the community. Throughout medical history, up to the passage of the National Research Act of 1974 in response to the Tuskegee syphilis study— in which six hundred low-income African American male sharecroppers in Macon County, Georgia, were provided "free medical care" that was a pseudonym for care that evaluated the outcomes of untreated syphilis over what was expected to be a six-month period but lasted thirty years—vulnerable populations have suffered maltreatment in the name of science without their consent. While

Tuskegee was the impetus for the National Research Act, other vulnerable populations had been targeted, including Jewish prisoners in concentration camps, slaves, children, those with mental illnesses, and prisoners.[8] With this history of mistreatment, RWJBH felt it incumbent to work with community partners, traditional and nontraditional, to forge real, meaningful alliances to build trust that has been broken over generations.

Finally, we are continually challenged with systemic issues that have resulted in the creation of a permanent underclass. While this is not unique to New Jersey or the RWJBH region, it is a challenge we have to look squarely in the face if we are to improve health outcomes, eliminate health disparities, and create true health equity. We spoke a little about the variability in household income and lifespan from one community to the next; however, similar health disparities are displayed among vulnerable populations that live even in the most affluent communities. For example, maternal mortality and infant mortality rates within minority communities, particularly among African Americans, remain significantly higher than those of their white counterparts, regardless of income, education, or lifestyle choices. This is due to a multitude of factors, including human bias and misconceptions, administrative procedures, and laws. While it is harder to tackle human bias, we can simultaneously work on strategic systems changes, partnering with our internal stakeholders and policy makers to address the policies and laws that were created in response to misconceptions.

Understanding the challenges, RWJBH steeled itself to catalyze

---

8   "History of Ethics," accessed Jan. 6, 2020, https://erau.edu/-/media/files/university/research/irb-history-of-ethics.pdf?la=en&hash=2AF300850C345B9F444ECFC95B92DD8F38FB6583.

its system and impact the communities in which it operates … but where would we begin?

DEANNA MINUS-VINCENT, VICE PRESIDENT OF SOCIAL IMPACT AND COMMUNITY INVESTMENT, RWJBARNABAS HEALTH

When you have an affiliated forty-four thousand employees and you're trying to change a mission, not everyone's going to get on board at the same time. For instance, when I first started talking about having a universally applied social determinant of health screening, some people said at first, "But how are we going to know who to ask?" We are going to ask everyone, because there is going to be implicit bias if you only ask some people. The fact is, the face of poverty is changing in this country and this state, where over 40 percent of our population can't meet their basic needs. That person you've been sitting down the pew from in church for years can't afford the same standard of living she had before. Now she may go home to nothing but a carton of milk in her refrigerator.

Addressing the Challenges: Where Do We Begin?

We knew we had a huge task ahead, but before jumping in we wanted to understand the scope of the problem, so we turned to the data. Our research covered not only data from each of our hospitals' community health needs assessments (CHNAs) but also data compiled by entities like the World Health Organization, the

Centers for Disease Control, the state department of health, and the Robert Wood Johnson Foundation, among others. What was already being done across the country in this space? We wanted to see what other healthcare systems as well as nonhealthcare entities were trying to accomplish in terms of social change. Where were the success stories, and what might we learn from the failures?

We were heartened to find that we weren't the only ones thinking in this way: in a publication entitled "Can Hospitals Heal Communities?" by Ted Howard (cofounder and president of the Democracy Collaborative) and Tyler Norris (formerly of Kaiser Permanente, currently chief executive of Well Being Trust), the question was, "How can hospitals utilize the breadth and depth of their essence in order to be about the business of aiding and assisting the community, rather than just being focused on the bottom line?"[9] There is such a direct correlation between housing and health that a healthcare system in Baltimore, Bon Secours, had erected senior housing units. And the Root Cause Coalition, cocreated by ProMedica and AARP, was doing important work at the intersection of healthcare, nonprofit organizations, and government to address food insecurity and other social determinants of health. ProMedica owns and operates its own supermarket because they understood that food is medicine and food insecurity and hunger are greater determinants of healthcare outcomes and contributors to reducing healthcare disparities than most people realize.

Traditionally, hospitals are hugely competitive, but this is the one space in which we have said, "Listen, if we remain so competi-

---

9   Tyler Norris and Ted Howard, "Can Hospitals Heal Communities?" Democracy Collaborative, accessed Sep. 6, 2019, https://democracycollaborative.org/content/can-hospitals-heal-americas-communities-0.

tive that we can't collaborate, then we have to realize we are contributing to the negative health outcomes that are prevalent in our communities"—and that wasn't what any of us wanted.

We knew we couldn't do everything all at once, so the questions became, "What are our inherent resources? What can we utilize in order to effectuate change in the areas of greatest need, as revealed by our community health needs assessment and discussions with our community advisory boards?" That wound up being our place-based presence and enhancing our commitment as an anchor institution. We could decide to hire differently, purchase goods differently, and invest in our community differently.

Taking that tack required a shift in the status quo. Those of us who work in these institutions generally pass through communities of vulnerable populations so impacted by societal benign neglect that many of them resemble battlefields. Once through these communities, we arrive at healthcare destinations and enter through shining glass doors into palatial facilities. As a result of this paradigm, there exists a heightened likelihood of disconnect between those making decisions and those for whom the decisions are being made.

If our quest was to eliminate healthcare disparities, clearly achieving health equity would require an institutional change in the way in which the power dynamic is characterized. What would make our work special/different/unique was the realization that the work had to be led by a commitment to change and that this commitment had to be viewed through a lens that seeks equity.

We didn't have to boil the ocean; we just had to be willing to address the poverty in our own backyard.

We didn't have to boil the ocean; we just had to be willing to address the poverty in our own backyard.

Even addressing the poverty in our own backyard seemed overwhelming. We knew we had many initiatives we could begin at the corporate level, such as altering our procurement efforts. We also knew we could work within each community to implement at least one social impact project, but where would we begin to tackle this effort in a comprehensive way? We knew we must start somewhere. After careful deliberation, Newark, New Jersey, became the natural fit. Not because there weren't other vulnerable communities across our footprint—there are vulnerable populations in every community—but because Newark presented a unique opportunity. Newark Beth Israel Medical Center, an RWJBH anchor institution, was already heavily entrenched in the community and had deep partnerships with community-based agencies, academia, and municipal government. Creating a healthier Newark would provide a win-win for everyone, especially its residents.

Newark, New Jersey, is located in Essex County and is 26.1 square miles. Despite being the state's largest city, "Brick City" suffered from the suburbanization movement of the 1960s and 1970s, especially after what is often called the Newark Rebellion, five days of violence that erupted on July 12, 1967, when rumors spread that police had arrested and killed a black cab driver. Across the country, in Los Angeles, Watts, and Detroit, as well as other areas of New Jersey, years of poverty, police brutality, and broken promises to inner-city residents had exploded into riots during the preceding weeks. The Newark Rebellion left the city in flames and further strained relations between city government, law enforcement, and the people of Newark. Twenty-six people were killed and more than seven hundred were injured, while damage to property was estimated at $10 million. White flight, which had already begun, was sped by the worry that things would get worse, and many businesses closed for good.[10]

Understanding the history of the city helps to better explain why, as a health system with a hospital there, RWJBH would ask, "What can we do in order to make certain we are trying to bring equity to a place with a history of disparate impact?" If you know that unemployed people are 54 percent more likely to be in poor or fair health and that the city of Newark's unemployment rate is 40 percent higher than the state's unemployment rate, you can't possibly expect the same health outcomes from that environment as you would other more resourced areas. Neither can you merely shrug it off, because if you're a large economic engine in the community, why aren't *you* hiring from that community? It's incorrect to presume that there's a skills deficit or skills gap in the community if you have never assessed it. We had to ask ourselves, "Is there actually a skills gap or is that an implicit bias belief? And if there is a gap, why aren't we working with the local schools to create a curriculum to eliminate that?"

These were the factors that led up to approaching what we as an institution could do to create sustainable, long-term systems change—not just a single initiative or one project, but addressing what it would take to lift up an entire community that has suffered benign neglect by disinvestment.

10   Rick Rojas and Khorri Atkinson. "50 Years After the Uprising: Five Days of Unrest That Shaped, and Haunted, Newark." *New York Times*. July 2017.

BUILDING THE CASE FOR CHANGE

Newark Beth Israel Medical Center's (NBIMC) 2016 Community Health Needs Assessment (CHNA)[11] gave us actionable insights into our community's needs. CHNA is required of all nonprofit hospitals and it provided a lengthy and detailed document with a very clear picture of the health challenges faced by the Newark community. The CHNA data at the time depicted:

- Both violent crime and homicide rates are higher than statewide rates and the county health rankings national benchmarks. In Essex County, the violent crime rate was 674/100,000, more than double the statewide rate. Essex County was ranked highest by county health rankings in violent crimes. In 2014, the number of violent crimes per 1,000 NBIMC residents was 11.1, nearly four times the state rate of 2.61.

- In 2014, the NBIMC service area teen birth rate (age 15–19) was 33.4/1,000, higher than the Essex County rate of 21.2/1,000 and more than double the New Jersey rate of 12.6/1,000.

- Despite decreasing since 2010, the 2012 Essex County black infant mortality rate (8.7/1,000) was higher than the rate for all other racial/ethnic groups in the county.

- Essex County and its major urban centers continue to have a higher percentage (42.7 percent) of housing built before

---

11   "Community Health Needs Assessment, 2016-2018," RWJBarnabas Health, accessed Jan. 6, 2020, www.rwjbh.org/images/hospital-locations/newark-beth-israel-medical-center/about/community%20health%20needs%20assessment/ RWJBarnabas-CHNA-NBIMC-12-2016.pdf.

1950 than exists statewide (25.6 percent). Housing stock built before 1950 is more likely to contain lead paint.

- The NBIMC Steering Committee considered secondary and qualitative data to determine seven top health issues based on capacity, resources, competencies, and needs specific to the populations it serves. The selected issues are within the hospital's purview, competency, and resources to impact the community in a meaningful manner. These include heart disease, cancer, violence, diabetes, asthma, dental conditions, and infant mortality.

HEART DISEASE: Heart disease is the leading cause of death for both men and women of most ethnicities, causing one in every four deaths in the United States. Some of the most prevalent types of heart disease include coronary artery disease, heart attack, heart failure, congenital heart diseases, and stroke.

- Heart disease is the leading cause of death in the nation, New Jersey, and Essex County.

- The Essex County 2013 heart disease age-adjusted mortality rate of 182.1/100,000 was higher than the statewide rate, the rate of surrounding counties, and the Healthy People 2020 target rate of 108.8/100,000.

- Considering the age-adjusted mortality rate (AAMR) for stroke by race and ethnicity, Essex County, like New Jersey and comparison counties, has the highest AAMR among Blacks.

CANCER AND SICKLE CELL DISEASE CANCER: Cancer is the second leading cause of death in the United States, causing approximately 1,600 deaths per day.

- Between 5–10 percent of all cancer cases can be attributed to genetic defects and the remaining 90–95 percent to environmental and lifestyle factors. While genetics like age and family history cannot be manipulated, most other major risk factors and lifestyle choices can be changed.

- Obesity increases the risk of several cancers; physical activity and nutritious eating can help bring about a healthy weight.

- Tobacco, asbestos, radiation (gamma and x-rays), the sun, and car exhaust fumes are well-known carcinogens. The rate of breast cancer is greatly increased when women have excess estrogen levels for a prolonged time period.

- The AAMR for cancer among Essex County Blacks decreased 8.7 percent from 189.5/100,000 in 2010 to 174.4/100,000 in 2013. The decrease for Essex County Whites during the same time period is approximately 50 percent more than the decrease for Essex County Blacks.

- The 2013 cancer incidence rate in Essex County (495.9/100,000) was at least three times higher than the Healthy People 2020 target rate (161.4/100,000).

VIOLENCE: The World Health Organization (WHO) defines violence as "the intentional use of physical force or power, threatened or actual, against oneself, another person, or against a group or community that either results in or has a high likelihood of resulting in injury, death, psychological harm, development, or deprivation." The WHO further categorizes violence into seven types: child abuse, elder abuse, sexual violence, intimate partner violence, youth violence, collective violence, and self-directed violence. All types of violence directly affect the health of their victims.

▫ Violence is a leading cause of death for African American and Latino males aged 15–24.

▫ The indirect effects of violence have been linked to chronic disease (heart disease, asthma, stroke, cancer, and more), mental health problems (PTSD, stress, anxiety, depression, and more), lower quality of life, and an increased risk of perpetrating violence.

▫ Women who are at risk for physical violence are also at risk for sexual violence. Violence at societal, community, relationship, or individual levels can exacerbate and perpetuate violent behaviors at other levels.

▫ Between 2010 and 2012, the violent crime rate in Essex County was 674/100,000. Violent crimes declined in Essex County but remain more than double the statewide rate (261/100,000) and ten times higher than the county health rankings national benchmark (59/100,000).

▫ In 2014, the Newark violent crime rate was 1,110/100,000, nearly four times the New Jersey rate of 261/100,000.

▫ The 2013 rate of substantiated child abuse/neglect in Newark is 16 percent, higher than the Essex County rate of 14 percent.

DIABETES: Diabetes is a disease in which blood glucose levels are too high due to abnormal levels of the hormone insulin. In type 1 diabetes, the body is not able to make insulin. In type 2 diabetes, the more common type, the body does not make or use insulin well. Without enough insulin, glucose stays in your blood. Over time, too much glucose in the blood can cause serious problems, damaging the eyes, kidneys, and nerves. Diabetes can also cause heart disease, stroke, and even the need to remove a limb. Pregnant women can get gestational diabetes.

- Overweight children with diabetes are at risk for serious complications including kidney disease, blindness, and amputations.

- Diabetes is the fifth leading cause of death in Essex County. When comparing diabetes age-adjusted mortality rate by race and ethnicity in Essex County, Blacks had the highest AAMR for diabetes, similar to the state of New Jersey.

- The AAMR for diabetes among Essex County Blacks declined 17.4 percent from 38.5/100,000 in 2011 to 31.8/100,000 in 2013, lower than statewide at 34.1/100,000 and Union County at 35.2/100,000.

- In the same time frame, the rate for Hispanics decreased 28.4 percent from 31.3/100,000 to 22.4/100,000, lower than New Jersey at 24.5/100,000.

- In 2014, diabetes was ranked as the eighth highest ambulatory care sensitive condition for which NBIMC service area adults utilized the emergency department.

ASTHMA: Asthma is characterized by inflammation of air passages resulting in a temporary narrowing of the airways that allow air to travel from the nose and mouth to the lungs. Asthma can be caused by exposure to inhaled allergens and irritants resulting in inflamed or constricted airways. Symptoms include wheezing, coughing, and tightness in the chest.

- Asthma accounts for one-quarter of all United States emergency department (ED) visits, 10 million outpatient visits and nearly 500,000 hospitalizations. Direct costs of care account for nearly $10 billion in expenditures. Another $8 billion are indirect costs due to lost earnings from death and disability.

- Increasing ethnic differences in asthma prevalence and morbidity and mortality are highly correlated with poverty, urban air quality, lack of patient education, and inadequate medical care. Risk factors for asthma attacks are allergens such as pollen, dust, animal dander, drugs, and food additives, as well as viral respiratory infections and physical exertion. In addition, insect stings and cockroaches are common allergies in urban areas.

▫ In 2014, asthma was the third most common ambulatory care sensitive condition for ED visits among children and adults in the county and patient service area.

▫ Asthma and COPD ranked among the top five conditions for inpatient ambulatory care sensitive condition admissions in Essex County.

INFANT MORTALITY: Over 23,000 infants in the United States died in 2014. Nearly six in every thousand babies born die in the US in the first year of life. Most deaths are the result of birth defects, preterm births, maternal complications of pregnancy, sudden infant death syndrome, or injuries.

▫ Despite decreasing since 2010, the 2012 Essex County black infant mortality rate of 6.4/100,000 was 25 percent higher than the Essex County overall rate of 4.8/100,000.

Making the Case

After nine months of research into the evidence basis for the business case, the institution had a strategic framework for how it would approach the work: a playbook that would help us to better socialize the "what" and "why" of the work. The playbook outlined a formula for addressing the greatest community needs based on our CHNA data; our patients' experiences; and input from our community advisory boards, our policy partners, and other experts—both in subject matter and in lived poverty experience.

But effecting change of the size and scope of an institutional mission required a great deal beyond a written playbook. It required a true socialization effort. Our president and CEO, Barry H. Ostrowsky, began this uphill battle by leading the charge himself. It was an impactful effort to usher in a systemwide town hall series where the new mission message was both advanced and advocated for; that well-considered approach left no room to question whether the organization was truly committed to this seismic shift. This message had to be voiced in board rooms, meeting rooms, clinical huddles, and cafeterias if it was going to work at all levels within and outside of RWJBH.

BARRY H. OSTROWSKY, PRESIDENT AND CEO, RWJBARNABAS HEALTH

I don't think you can roll this out and then just expect it to self-execute. I think you have to bring in colleagues on a regular basis, talk about it, and reinforce the commitment we have. As one of the mechanisms for addressing these social determinants, we have chosen to have our institutions serve as anchor institutions in their communities. Once upon a time, you were an anchor institution if you were just there long enough; we've been in a number of our sites for a hundred-plus years, providing great clinical care, and before what I consider to be a new definition of an anchor institution, we'd considered ourselves an anchor institution. Same place, new buildings, new people, but we've been there. Now we were saying, "That's no longer an acceptable definition for an anchor institution."

> An anchor institution, in addition to its core business, has to invest in things like economic development, and in our case, these social determinant programs. Just being around a long time isn't sufficient. Being around and doing things in addition to your core product line, for the benefit of the community, is what in my view really defines you as an anchor institution.

That was the beginning—but we had a long, long way to go.

GUIDELINES FOR THE CHANGE AGENT

- As important as it is, inspiration can't replace perspiration; recognizing and naming the challenge is only the start.

- Make your case; do your research. There will be questions you need to have answered before they're asked: among them, "Why should we do this?" "How can this be done?" "Who else is doing it?" "What about our bottom line?" The answer "because it's the right thing to do" may be what motivates you, but you can't assume that's going to be enough for everyone whose support you'll need. You need to present a sound business plan.

- In making your case, be sure to include examples of failures of similar initiatives, along with success stories. You need to let your stakeholders see that you're approaching this from a realistic and knowledgeable place, not just cheerleading or cherry-picking data.

- Create and hone your narrative—and be prepared to tell your story to multiple stakeholders in language they'll understand.

If you can't make people understand the problem and your path to a solution, you won't get buy-in.

- Don't try to boil the ocean. You can't solve every problem with one initiative, but you can begin to make a change in one small area that can ripple out. Success breeds more success, so focus on what's within your purview.

- Be prepared to find that others have different ideas about what's important or what problems need addressing. Some may see it as a kind of competition. Find a way to reassure them that as the effort broadens, they'll be invited to be a part of it.

- Those same people may start naysaying your work before it begins in an effort to undermine you. Keep moving forward and don't get enmeshed in their machinations.

- Find both like-minded people and organizations in your community, or across the country if you have to, who are invested in solving the same problems and *listen* to them. You'll build valuable partnerships, get better insights, and glean ideas for how to proceed successfully (while dodging some potholes that others hit along the way).

- You need allies within your organization—but don't assume that buy-in from a higher-up means you're automatically cleared to bring on the winds of change. There are many more hurdles ahead, and you're going to be telling that story many, many times.

CHAPTER TWO

Turning the Ship

C hange agents within organizations need to be aware of the current culture they seek to change and must be meticulous about connecting all the dots for the team members less familiar with or more resistant to this work.

Communicating the work to others is central to creating an environment in which all participate and everyone is given a chance to win. From the beginning, you must have a communication strategy in place for your internal audience so they can better understand and embrace this work. This begins with the creation of a communications toolkit that offers clear, straightforward language to explain your mission shift and new commitment. Equip your executive senior leadership with the created toolkit. Give them examples, early and often, on how anchor mission-driven social impact and community investment can positively impact health outcomes, how the evidence illustrates that it's a way to get ahead of the cost curve of care delivery, and how it has been modeled, whether across the country or across the globe. Most importantly, provide them with the "why"—why we are doing this work, why this work matters, and why we need to be the ones to make the change. Being able to supply them with the appropriate language during the earliest stages of the process would have helped us to usher in what was going to become a major cultural shift within the organization. Note, your communications team may want to postpone or skip the "why" phase, as it requires quantifiable numbers, research, or anecdotal data. Do not do this. Internal storytelling will be pivotal in gaining the momentum that shall be required when budget dedication and FTE allotment discussions will need to be held. You can indeed build the plane as you fly it, and don't let anyone tell you that you cannot.

DARRELL TERRY, PRESIDENT AND CEO, NEWARK BETH ISRAEL MEDICAL CENTER AND CHILDREN'S HOSPITAL OF NEW JERSEY

Newark Beth Israel has historically done a lot of different things in the community. We have our own health fair, we participate in other organizations' health fairs, we have a men's health day, a women's health day; those kinds of events have been a staple at Newark Beth Israel during my time here, and that's been great. But when you look at the impact, when you look at the metrics, we haven't really been moving the needle. In Newark and Essex Counties you still see some of the worst outcomes. So, although it may benefit the few individuals who are participating in those events, it wasn't anything that was sustainable or something that was really having an impact on improving the health status or quality of life of the larger population. When Michellene introduced the social impact community investment concept to us, it was a whole new framework for us.

Understand Where Resistance Is Coming From

There are natural strategic tensions to doing this work. It is easy to inadvertently counter an attempt to procure locally with the aim of benefiting from economies of scale and vending solely through a group purchasing organization (GPO). Hence, in erecting an internal infrastructure to do this work, asset leaders must be empowered as the industry experts that they are. Leadership needs to hear that, coupled with the message of change: "You are the internal expert. I appreciate and respect what you bring to this table. We want to share with you some of what we've seen across the nation as best practices in this space. We ask that you be willing to work together so that we can begin turning our institutional ship in the direction of ensuring that we are setting public goals and aligning internal policies."

We will talk more about the strategy of forming what we call a corporate anchor roundtable later in this book, but whatever form or name you give your internal product line leadership group or anchor collaborative, soliciting their input and acknowledging their expertise and efforts are both critical to gaining and keeping their active support and enthusiasm for the work.

Utilize Allies Already Doing the Work as Ambassadors to Your Institution

It's instructive for a change agent to get a sense of what putting these new concepts and ideas into practice looks like. It sounds so simple on the page, but it required a lot of internal education to get people in human resources (HR), for example, to understand the how and why of local hiring. Johns Hopkins was already doing good work in the space, so we established a contact there and put our HR team in touch with them. It's hugely helpful when people have been used to doing what they do in a particular way—in this case, hiring—to be able to observe and learn from peers in other institutions who have already adopted and adapted to the kinds of local hiring practices and workforce development practices we were putting in place.

To help with compliance and clarity around the shift from business as usual to making a concerted effort to hire individuals who reflected the communities we serve, we appointed a member of the SICI team to oversee all of our anchor work. Diana Ortiz-Candelejo, director of anchor strategy for the SICI practice, worked with HR to make certain that we weren't just looking at entry-level jobs, but at jobs with promotion opportunities for a livable wage. That's an important aspect of ending the cycle of intergenerational poverty. She helps make sure that the intent of the work is carried forward and that we analyze the data we're capturing so we can measure how we're doing. Are our programs working, are we retaining participants, and are the policies we have in place helping them? How can we make certain there is fairness and equity in our quest to hit our goals? We were, however, gifted with great HR leadership; our CHRO, Marty Everhart, has demonstrated full commitment.

We were fortunate that right before our larger system merger, we had acquired a Hudson County hospital, Jersey City Medical Center. Jersey City Medical Center has something called the Career Ladders program, developed by Lourdes Valdes, director of workforce development and grants. Career Ladders creates opportunities within the institution that combine coaching and career planning, along with some onsite training and tuition support. It's a way to make sure frontline employees have the opportunity to obtain stackable certifications and encouragement to grow while moving up through the ranks. Their experience afforded us insights into how that kind of program could work at other institutions throughout our system. Our CHRO was wise enough to elevate Lourdes to the system office to scale the Career Ladders program across the System.

At Newark Beth Israel Medical Center, we began the Hire Newark Bootcamp in collaboration with Mayor Ras J. Baraka's Centers of Hope initiative, created for the long-term unemployed who are the most difficult to employ. How could we give them both marketable skills and soft skills to get them ready to reenter the workforce? Participants had been unemployed and underemployed for a long time, thanks to the recession, which in urban areas was more like a depression. How could we connect them with social services and put a cohort around them to help get them to bootcamp every day? Accountability helps develop a culture of teamwork, so it becomes, "I need to hold up my end of the bargain so that other folks in my cohort are not negatively impacted."

Currently, we're working with our first four classes of hires to help them grow in the jobs they have now and move up within the institution. What additional training or support do they need in order to become viable candidates for promotional opportunities? What additional soft skills would enhance their employability? Again, the work invokes a design methodology, so we're able to review and alter initiatives along the way based on what we learn alongside participants. Darrelle Terry, NBIMC CEO, utilized this design when he aptly halted recruiting new classes of participants and instead opted to work more poignantly with graduates of the program to ensure their success.

We did not hire all of these people ourselves. We contacted other businesses throughout the city and said, "We're going to be training these folks and hope that you would be open to taking them on board as new employees. What we will guarantee you is that they receive training, and we invite you to help cocreate this curriculum so that we're giving you a member of the workforce you're going to want to keep."

BARRY H. OSTROWSKY, PRESIDENT AND CEO, RWJBARNABAS HEALTH

Our bootcamp is nine weeks of training that starts with the questions "How do you dress for an interview? How do you act in an interview for a job?" and goes straight through to graduation, when every member of the graduating class gets a job, from our organization or others. We've had four graduations to date, and at each graduation, we not only have members of the graduating class speak, but we typically bring back previous graduates, who tell the story of what's happened since they graduated. And we're delighted to hear that not only did people get entry-level jobs but a number of them have already gotten promotions and have made themselves more successful. That's the kind of highlighting I think makes a lot of difference, and it creates this kind of relationship where the graduates of one class will be mentors to others who come out of the next class, and folks in their place of employment are typically mentoring them as they've come through this track.

Dealing with the Unknown

In order to usher in mission change, accountability is required. The institution must hold itself and its various asset leaders accountable. To help advance and track our anchor work as well as mitigate challenges in asset leaders' respective areas, we have requested they provide the SICI team with impact reports (examples provided in the appendix). These quarterly reports help us document our progress and barriers over time and will help us create a dashboard of our collective impact.

Asset leaders are encouraged to have their departmental liaisons complete the reports based on the projects they oversee and can provide greater detail. It's optimal that asset leaders will have several initiatives that contribute to our anchor buy, hire, and invest local strategy, and we may receive several reports from separate departmental liaisons for one department. That's because while information technology, marketing, treasury, pharmacy, and human resources may each have a social impact initiative unique to them—like mentoring new urban tech firms at a local incubator by IT or the pharmacy's Dispensary of Hope initiative to supply no-cost and low-cost medications to the most vulnerable patients—each department is mandated to use every opportunity to utilize a small, local, minority, or woman- or veteran-owned business as a part of our ongoing commitment to our anchor mission.

The individual tracking of local spend and hiring allows us to be able to attribute department-specific efforts, since we also track system-level local hiring and procurement. Therefore, we are able to keep asset leaders accountable during each quarterly corporate anchor roundtable (CAR) meeting to recognize their individual contributions. We recognize that both quantitative and qualitative measures are valuable indicators of progress, so the impact statements required include a written narrative section as well as Excel spreadsheets for numerical reporting.

In our local hire effort, we measure total Newark hires by race, gender, full-time/part- time/average hourly wages, job titles, and retention rate. Other measurements include interns from specific zip codes as well as partnerships and collaborations with community-based organizations and institutions. We measure total local and diverse spend based on shared definitions that have been developed by supply chain, SICI, and legal counsel in concert with state and federal standards and adopted by the system. Indicators are continually refined and analyzed to determine which ones require further exploration to identify trends.

Once we obtain impact reports from asset leaders, the SICI anchor director works with them to address clarifying questions and acquire more details to verify that their efforts indeed count as local hiring and local procurement. Where necessary, we will provide recommendations and direction to help enhance their projects and ensure mission alignment (whether it be metrics, community partners to include, diversity vendor verification, or definitions). For example, upon first launch some asset leaders had difficulty embracing the place-based focus of our work. As a result, some would attempt to assert spend with national minority-owned businesses. Doing so may be easier but it flies in the face of this work, as spend with a diverse supplier in Michigan or Illinois does nothing to create economic stimulus in the communities in which our hospitals sit. An additional example was the counting of an internship opportunity given to nontraditional out-of-state students. While both efforts may be worthy in their own right, the director of anchor strategy helps to deepen understanding and enhance compliance to our local anchor strategy.

Impact reports are assessed each quarter before CAR meetings, with special attention and technical assistance given to those asset leaders who are expected to present at the upcoming CAR meeting.

Other outcomes not necessarily captured in these reports but promoted through the SICI and policy and government affairs team in collaboration with the legal team is the internal policy reforms and systems change necessary to enable our hire, buy, and invest local strategy. The impact reports allow us to become aware of internal barriers that can hinder or delay anchor efforts, which in turn helps us to determine appropriate internal policies and practices that need to be altered to be more inclusive.

Change is hard, and the unknown is that much more so. As organizational winds shift, there may be the tendency to minimize a monumental effort. This was evidence-based work, because our research had confirmed its efficacy and value, but this is where the need for personal resiliency—to put it bluntly, a thick skin—comes in. Your team needs to understand that they too may experience immense institutional resistance that is natural with organizational transition and transformation. Change can be scary. Different is often rejected. You don't know what's on the other side. Many relied heavily upon our CEO's assured certainty that we were heading in the right direction and that just because it was hard did not mean we were going to abandon ship. When it feels as if you are experiencing pushback on all sides, can you imagine how horrible it would be to have your organization change course midstream? The support of the CEO and board were invaluable.

You won't be able to rally everyone, certainly not initially—but don't let your efforts get sidetracked. Do we want to create a tent that's large enough to bring other folks along? Certainly. But don't get pulled off course by the distraction of the resistant naysayer. It may be natural to spend time trying to hush the whisper campaigns or putting out the little fires that may get fanned in an attempt to divert attention, but it isn't useful and can run the risk of not getting anything else done. Distraction comes to derail you, and that can be fatal. As we saw it, the need in our communities was so vast and deep that we could not afford to be deterred.

the need in our communities was so vast and deep that we could not afford to be deterred.

Everyone has their own duties and responsibilities. They are on task to fulfill that which their job requires, and you may come along with a "how-to" flag they weren't looking for. There may be some who just won't make an effort to understand or buy into what you are trying to do or how it could work—and that's okay. Resistance is natural. Don't take it personally. Realize now that they'll get there once everyone else gets there and once a few wins are realized. There are those who are naturally intellectually curious and others who are less so. Be prepared to understand that the demands on their time may not permit them to read what you give them, anyway, so they have to be shown your proof of concept in action. They'll come around, or they won't— but you can't let yourself be sidetracked trying to win everyone over at the start.

SARAH LECHNER, SENIOR VICE PRESIDENT FOR POLICY DEVELOPMENT AND GOVERNMENT AFFAIRS AT RWJBARNABAS HEALTH AND CHIEF OF STAFF TO THE SOCIAL IMPACT AND COMMUNITY INVESTMENT PRACTICE

There are a lot of changes at the federal and state levels with how healthcare operates and how it's financed. And many healthcare systems and hospitals, including ours, are pursuing both horizontal and vertical integration. So there are certainly some within our system who believe that clinical work is our core mission and these potential changes require the system to double down on that work. There were others within the system who believed that the work was not sustainable; that there's no a short-term or long-term ROI and therefore it isn't something that the system should be pursuing.

Those sentiments have decreased, particularly as we've integrated the practice into the system's mission and strategic plan. And we had some quick wins, which helped turn the tide as well.

The fundamental premise of our practice is to ensure the health and well-being of our communities. And when you hear our CEO talk about how the system is—and should be—a social service organization, not a hospital organization, it inherently makes sense to some; but it doesn't to everyone within the system. And that's okay. It's definitely a process, and our core SICI team needed to understand that not everyone within our system would naturally embrace our work. It's been a journey—and a learning experience—to figure out how to explain this practice, why it's critical to our communities, and how everyone can play a role.

We were getting no resistance from outside the organization, largely due to our record of traditional nonprofit hospital community benefit work and the relationships formed with those at the community, municipal, state, and federal levels. On the contrary, they were interested, were welcoming, and wanted to get on board and partner with us. How could they help? What role could they play in expanding and accelerating the work to better our communities?

For our policy leaders, we explained that the effort was going to be policy led and that they'd have significant roles in helping reform policy to support our anchor and SICI efforts, that we would need everything from primary sponsors to cosponsors on legislation or for them to evidence their support of certain amendments to existing statutes or to pass municipal resolutions. They were all in. We implored our community-based organizations and resident partners to educate us on what the felt needs of their constituents were and to help identify the barriers to access that existed through state and federal laws, polices, regulations, and rules that kept their communities from thriving. We then asked that they avail themselves as expert storytellers of their own experiences as we worked alongside them to advise elected officials and agency leaders on the ways to remove these barriers or to eliminate, rather than merely fill, the gaps that created inequities and contributed to disparities.

Why the enthusiasm? We think it was in large part because while most people see the problems in society, the default mode is to look to government to fix things—yet here was a corporate entity, a healthcare entity, coming forward and saying we understood that there was a level of accountability we all share in this space and we wanted to be a part of changing things. We weren't bringing them a problem; we were bringing our data and ideas forward as solutions, a way in which we could all work better together. On our side, we wanted to work with their constituents in a very real and dynamic way and to share what we'd heard from them in a manner that would help these legislators better understand their needs.

They welcomed the opportunity to extend their thought leadership and to have an ally in our sector committed to creating change. For once, they weren't tasked with riding to the rescue; we were asking them whether we could be part of the cavalry.

A second part had to do with the fact that RWJBH is a well-known, well-respected healthcare entity in the state. We'd been involved in our local communities for years as a traditional not-for-profit hospital serving the community, so it wasn't a question of them seeing new faces popping up at meetings. The difference now was that we were seeking to do something differently than we had been, to be truly innovative with our resources—employees, operations, partnership, and process.

No matter what work you're doing or what you're trying to accomplish, getting buy-in from both those inside and outside of your organization is critical to your success—and that rests on your ability and willingness to communicate your direction clearly, consistently, and often in language they understand. It also requires that you listen actively and provide them an opportunity to codesign with you.

GUIDELINES FOR THE CHANGE AGENT

- It's critical that you are prepared to meet those to whom you're bringing change where they are—whether that's within your organization or outside of it.

- Do you understand what those who are tasked with maintaining your organization's fiscal health are likely going to be most concerned about regarding any change and its impact on the bottom line? Help them to see the value of the work you're doing through *their* lens; don't expect them to view it through yours. Be prepared to present your initiative in their language; for example, with finance utilize the organization's fiscal mandate, goals, and targets. Be sensitive to their role in the organization There *is* a powerful business case for this work, and you need to be able to make it, whether that's to the financial officer or to HR.

- Be ready to connect people in your organization with senior leaders at other similar organizations, where the kind of change you're promoting is already in place. We were able to connect several of our asset leaders, through the HAN, with counterparts at other hospitals, and the discussions they had proved tremendously helpful in getting buy-in for the work. Use your network and leverage that in order to find out who they respect in their own industry, then have those folks to connect with them.

- Value peoples' time as much as they do; get your talk down to an elevator pitch. People are busy—be mindful of the impact of your ask on their time and to-do list. For example, if you're taking up too much of their time, they're not going to feel respected. Lack of feeling respected often results in rejection. Understand that you're asking them to spend brain bandwidth as well as learn a new concept. Be cautious of spending too much time on the big picture when what they need to know is what is required of *them* and what are the immediate steps for *them* to take toward success.

- Make sure you have something tangible to offer beyond your change agenda: "You're having difficulty recruiting in a particular space? I know several top professional recruiters and I'm happy to connect you to them. Do we anticipate a future need for hiring in this nontraditional role? I'm on the board of several higher educational institutions, I'd be happy to put you in touch with their presidents and deans to discuss curriculum development." Don't go in empty-handed, asking for things; have something to offer that makes their job easier or solves an existing challenge.

- Create a safe space for yourself and practice self-care; you're going to have to show up for your institution and your team before you know how this is all going to turn out, and your resilience will be sorely tried. Give yourself some grace; get yourself a "kitchen cabinet" of people whom you trust, and with whom you can have vulnerable conversations in complete and utter confidence—preferably people *outside* of your organization. Provide yourself the opportunity to express natural frustrations and be encouraged and built back up. Preserve your humanity; your compassion and empathy for others is made stronger through your own challenge experiences.

CHAPTER THREE

Launching a League of Leaders

Y ou can't do this work alone—and you shouldn't even try. It's not a one-man or one-woman show. It's critical to have others on board with you to take on the task, in no small part because they become a team of allies and ambassadors as they experience the challenges of making change along with you. That requires you to be a leader of leaders—and to relinquish power to them. This work, when done well, diffuses power from the traditional hierarchical organization chart and spreads it throughout the team.

How do we empower people? Begin with information; share as much of it as you have regarding the why and how of the project, obviously, but beyond that be candid from the start about the level of resistance they should expect. People don't love being managed, but they do gravitate to leadership. We call our team of corporate and hospital SICI leaders a "league of leaders." We are each codesigning innovative solutions to the work, but it is done while adhering to a team charter that aims to break down silos and check egos at the door so that the "all" can win.

How you lead in this effort is as important as *whom* you lead: Do you provide them with access and opportunity? Do you encourage them to lean in with all of their creative and innovative skills, talents, and abilities, whether or not those are the same ones typically tapped by their job description? Are you providing them with opportunities to cocreate some elements with you? It's not just about having helpers on board; you've got to give them some creative freedom and real, meaningful opportunities to shine on their own, in the hopes of developing ownership of the work and its outcomes. You're asking them to be ambassadors for an unknown country. It's like asking people who've never seen rain to throw their work and support into building an ark. That's why it's important to lead in a way that builds trust, rather than simply flexing your authority. Yet, there's balance to this—not everyone adapts to new knowledge at the same rate. So while you wish to empower, ensure that they are transparent about how they are invoking the new change principles into their work as well.

Model a leadership style that values transparency. Be willing to show some level of vulnerability. Does that mean you are called upon to walk into a team meeting and fall apart? Of course not. But it is okay to say to them "I don't know" or "Let's figure that out together" when that's the truth. Like the work itself, this requires a leap of faith on your part and theirs, so you need individuals who themselves are not afraid to be unicorns—to stand out as different from the majority of others within your organization.

> ## SARAH LECHNER, SENIOR VICE PRESIDENT FOR POLICY DEVELOPMENT AND GOVERNMENT AFFAIRS AT RWJBARNABAS HEALTH AND CHIEF OF STAFF TO THE SOCIAL IMPACT AND COMMUNITY INVESTMENT PRACTICE
>
> We've really emphasized, on our team, a lack of hierarchy. We have people who are responsible and accountable for projects, but given the depth and breadth of all of our experiences, both professionally and lived, it's a really nice blend for everyone to collaborate and codesign.

What Kinds of People Should You Enlist?

When we were choosing people for our team, part of it was thinking strategically; do the areas of their specialties lend themselves to social impact work? Are they imaginative and intellectually curious? Some individuals are drawn to being lifelong learners; nearly all of those on this team certainly are. Your league of leaders needs to have an intellectually inquisitive life beyond the specialty of their field, and you should be able to see evidence of that.

For instance, one of the members of our team is also an elected official in her hometown, which shows community commitment and intellectual curiosity. Another is an avid justice artist, a painter who serves as president of a local community art and social justice organization. Another is a volunteer fireman in his town and our director for global health/chief medical officer for social impact and an OB/GYN; he and his wife (a head of cardiology in a completely different healthcare system) also lead a global health nonprofit. Yet another volunteers in her community nearly every day and works almost seven days per week. These are people with breadth, depth, energy, and imagination, the ones who realize, "There's more inside of me to give, and more that the world needs done."

Our SVP of healthy living and community wellness, Barbara Mintz, jokingly refers to us as the "Social Impact Justice League," but it's really about team members' eagerness to use all the gifts and talents they have, not just the ones drawn upon by their job descriptions. That brings them to the work and makes them persistent enough to be great at it. We didn't need the person whose attitude is "I'm only here to do my job" or the one that said, "requiring us to be transparent and codesign our work outside of silos is micromanaging." We needed the person who was new to the space and said, "I know this is the way it's been done here, but I've researched it and in the systems across the globe in the Netherlands or across the country in San Francisco, they've done it better," and wanted to share that big idea. Too often, people who are innovative and curious have that stifled in their day jobs, because they're afraid they're going to be looked at negatively, laughed at, or told to keep their comments to themselves. If we can get to those folks before they become conditioned not to be themselves, then we can really make a win. It has been stated that change can be scary for many. We need those who were okay to say, "I'm scared, but I am willing to try anyway!" Do it scared. Go beyond your comfort zone. An environment that tolerates risk is imperative to fostering creativity, and creativity is a prerequisite for social change.

People like these are your intrapreneurs—your inside change agents, with the vision and energy you and they will need to bring about organizational social innovation change, because this work is not about hoarding power at the top; it's about dispersing power, then codesigning a platform forward.

That flies in the face of how things are traditionally run in the healthcare industry, or any other large-scale corporate entity, which tends to be very hierarchical. We are uniquely positioned because we have a CEO who seeks out and welcomes diversity of thought and representation and doesn't care about the title attached to a novel idea.

Your league of leaders knows the realities of the organization they are in, which is why it's important to tell them, "Listen, we're going to have a team charter, because everyone gets empowered around this table. We need to make certain your voices are heard and that your fingerprints are on the work we are doing and how it's being built." This message has to trickle down to the people on their teams, too, because again, we're talking about a massive cultural shift—the turning of the ship—not a one-off effort.

As your work progresses and people begin to buy in, you may also enjoy the confidence and help of people we call "secret agents"; those who may hear about resistance from within their department or another division and who will offer their insight and wisdom in conflict resolution in order to assist in advancing the work. These agents show up all over the place, from management to frontline staff to clinicians, and they'll be an invaluable asset to you.

Success breeds success and has many fathers; failure is an orphan.

As your effort gains momentum, you'll find people coming to you with ideas, with offers of help, and with valuable insights on where resources for the work might be found, out of their own expertise. Success breeds success and has many fathers; failure is an orphan. Given a track record of success, even those who were initially on the sidelines will begin to come forward.

As your team grows, no one person is going to have ownership of any single area or idea, and people who are used to ceding some responsibility, to needing to trust and rely on others, will become more comfortable with that and require less handholding. You're partners, not competitors, in this effort—like members of an orchestra, each is a highly skilled and practiced expert. And even though there may be a cacophony at the beginning when everyone's tuning up, once the orchestra conductor raises the baton, they've all got to play harmoniously together from the same sheet of music.

MICHELLENE DAVIS, EXECUTIVE VICE PRESIDENT AND CHIEF CORPORATE AFFAIRS OFFICER, RWJBARNABAS HEALTH

For some people—those who are too deeply invested in ego, in titles, in hierarchy and the status quo—this kind of teamwork just isn't going to be a good fit. That goes, too, for those who are frightened or threatened by any kind of upheaval or change. You can't always see that initially, but it will show itself eventually, and you've got to be prepared to move people out if they're finding it too challenging. I've seen this kind of internal resistance come from different people with various kinds of issues; in one case, it was an ingrained lack of flexibility. But in any case, the whole of the work requires the leader to assess whether this team player is willfully causing obstruction or whether they are just learning to adapt to the change at a different pace.

Sometimes the internal resistance is linked to what the individual's worldview is, based on who they are and what their life experience is, and if that surfaces as hostility to the work—and it can—you've got to root it out without hesitation. There are people who will tell you that the poor have brought their status on themselves, who don't understand or acknowledge the systemic and structural inequity of policy that has existed in this country and enabled the proliferation of an underclass. They don't understand the disenfranchised, they don't empathize, and on some level, they find any challenge to that worldview a personal threat. Do not be naïve about that. This work is focused on achieving equity—and as such, forces you to call out the systemic and structural classism within the underpinnings of society.

In the law, there is something called the eggshell theory, which means you take your victims as you find them. Similarly, you take your team members as you find them. As the change agent, you have to be emotionally intelligent enough to recognize when stuff gets kicked up and some red flags are raised. For some, that's when I hear the underlying "blame the victim" message and I know this person doesn't really understand the problem, much less how a large-scale organization may have contributed to that problem over time and as such can be a viable solution to solving it. You can't allow that in, because if they're not genuinely invested in equity-seeking work, they will undermine your efforts and those of the rest of the team. Afford them an opportunity to learn, invest in them by providing an equity coach, even, but when undermining activity is repeated, be fair to the work of the team and make the hard decision to grant them the chance to explore a different career path.

BARRY OSTROWSKY, PRESIDENT AND CEO, RWJBARNABAS HEALTH

What I've said to the management team is, "Look, I'm committed for a variety of reasons to our programs that address social determinants. If you're not motivated to do that because of morality, or because you think it's the right thing to do, or because you're tired of hearing people suffering unnecessarily, if none of that moves you to do it, then—looking at the macro system or healthcare system—if we don't stop folks coming for conventional clinical care because we fail to address these social determinants, eventually the entire system will run out of resources and the clinical care we give will sink to a lower common denominator. So if we're ultimately successful in the social determinant side, that's going to prevent the development of unnecessary illness and conditions. It'll stop disproportionality, certainly in our vulnerable communities, and as a result, fewer folks will now come to get clinical services, which will reduce the burden on resources for clinical services, and we'll have more resources to truly address the needs of people who are sick and whose illnesses we couldn't prevent, and so we won't have to reduce qualitatively the kind of services we provide."

As far as I'm concerned, people may reject both motivations, but I think if doing "the right thing" for people in need just isn't something that resonates, if you're serious about protecting access to quality healthcare, you should be motivated in that regard, because we have far too many people getting sick unnecessarily.

Setting Goals

How do you set goals for your team for what needs to be accomplished by the individuals and by the team as a whole? When you're working with a league of leaders, the goals are set in concert with them, because if not, they're arbitrary and capricious rather than meaningful and real.

It's the same thing for our asset leaders: we do not go to them and simply dictate, "10 or 20 percent of our overall spend has to be done with local diverse suppliers." You've got to work *with* them: "So talk to us; what are our greatest trends in our spend areas? Where do we see opportunity? What's outside of our group purchasing organization, and can we grow that? If we can identity entities within our footprint who provide that service or product you need, can we connect these two dots in order to create a continuous and recurring spend?"

Goal setting can often be a formula but, in this space, it must also be customizable: it's not X plus Y equals Z as much as it is the fact that goal setting must be done with the asset leader, with the team member, or else you run the risk of losing them. Dictating the goal flies in the face of what this work is supposed to look like, which is codesigning.

They Are Sharing the Load—Let Them Share the Successes Too

Your team will be dealing with naysayers just as you will; they'll be hearing the whispers, seeing the doubt and political maneuvering that change flushes out in an organization. Make certain that your team is supported and that their confidence is shored up, because in the early stages of doing the change work, the naysaying will reach its crescendo, so your team must be comprised of individuals who don't give way to that. You don't want folks running back to you to share breathless reports on office gossip around your efforts, because they should know that you don't and can't care about it. They should be feeling established enough in the work to understand that "this is not about us. This is about the work we are doing." Keep the rumor mill at bay to the extent that you can and discourage people from sharing it.

Work with people closely on the establishment of their initiatives, giving way to their expertise and holding them up and out. Aim to leverage the initiative's position in the organization in order to give them the spotlight and opportunity to shine, especially after they have worked on something then brought it to you to help get it over the goal line. Your team member should have an opportunity to enjoy the success and recognition they deserve.

When You Have a Hammer...

...Every problem can look like a nail. Similarly, when you have experts from different disciplines seated at your table, there can be a tendency for each of them to see a particular problem or its solution filtered solely through their own special expertise. Make a conscious effort to get people to address things in an interdisciplinary way. We don't want the person who specializes in policy to explain the policy ramifications of local hiring: we want the person who oversees local hiring to explain the policy ramifications around local hiring and the person who oversees food security to explain how housing impacts health. That creates a layer of cross-disciplin-ary training, tracking, and ability.

You don't have to be a deep-sea diver in every single area, but you've got to be able to go more than just surface-deep in order to bring value to that space. That means the procurement person needs to be able to address the importance of utilizing local procurement in order to encourage local hiring and then the financial implica-tions of local investment, for instance, and eventually how efforts around economic development correlate with efforts on community wellness. Everyone needs to be conversant with how the work of one impacts the work of the other. The person who is doing housing can speak to healthy housing through a redevelopment lens, but she also has to be able to make the case around why healthy homes matter through community wellness and wealth-building perspectives.

Make sure, too, that your people are self-starters, ready and able to roll up their sleeves. You need to invest in building up the resil-iency of your team, as you will need people who can bounce back, figure it out, and move forward. Not all leaders may want that; some people are happiest telling others what to do, but you don't have to have all the answers and you don't have to pretend that you do.

Look for kindness in your team members. It's challenging work already, and sharp elbows don't make it easier. We understand ambition, and we understand having an appetite for the fray, but if you can't be kind, embracing, and innovative simultaneously, this isn't the place for you. Leadership needs to set the tone and tenor for the rules of engage-ment very clearly, and those rules apply to everyone.

And please, don't forget that even as you're changing the world, life goes on. Make certain that you're checking in with your team to see how they're doing psychologically, because we all have challenges beyond the workplace that may not be evident to our colleagues but that can really rock our personal worlds. One of our team members suffered a personal health issue; another's spouse received a grave medical diagnosis. Life happens, so make certain that you create an environment that deals with them as people.

When the personalities are well matched and everyone's pulling in the same direction, you can accomplish great things—things that couldn't have been done had just one kind of expertise or personality been tapped. Seek out your league of leaders, empower them with your trust, educate them about your effort, and inspire them to join forces. Together, you will move mountains.

Be cautious of the quest to fill the trenches with those who are a good "culture fit." Historically, "culture fit" is code for lack of diversity; diversity of thought, perspective, ethnicity, race, sexual preference, and lived experience. Surrender this tendency; diversity makes your team, and thus your work, stronger—embrace it.

GUIDELINES FOR CHANGE AGENTS

- This kind of work can't be done solo. You need a team—a league of leaders—who are invested in the mission and in bringing both their expertise and intellectual curiosity to the table.

- Look for the imaginative, the energetic, and the innovative when you're seeking out team members. You don't want people who are too invested in the status quo; you need those who aren't afraid to ask questions or try a new path and are self-motivated to learn a new way of doing and being. Be patient. Change can be scary; not everyone will rush to jump into the deep end. But the change agent-to-be will muster the courage and come around.

- Don't simply dictate, to your team or your asset leaders. Remember, the work needs to be collaborative, and you're working with leaders, not followers. That's a source of strength.

- Do share the spotlight and any opportunity for recognition with those whose work has supported a successful initiative. Recognize that everyone wants to be a part of the win.

- Empower your team with access, information, and responsibility.

- Encourage everyone on the team to get out of their silos and learn to see the problem through others' perspectives. Problems are most effectively solved when they're approached from a multidisciplinary perspective.

- Choose people whose personalities are collegial, not overtly competitive. In this atmosphere, everyone wins by pulling together.

- Don't get so wrapped up in your mission that you forget that they, like you, have a lives outside of the work to deal with. Encourage them to have fuller, bigger lives. Change agency requires a resiliency that is best bolstered by balanced support.

CHAPTER FOUR

Outside In and Inside Up –Building a More Inclusive Environment

What's the value to a change agent's agenda in bringing in community stakeholders and others from outside of your organization to advise you in shaping your work and goals? In our view, what you are trying to change are systems and structures that have traditionally been created without the input of the individuals they affect. Thus, you want to be more inclusive, more deliberate, and more thoughtful in your approach.

You need to give the community stakeholders, whose environment you hope to influence, alter, or benefit, an opportunity for buy-in, awareness, design, reflection, and education—or more accurately, for coeducation. You want to see their fingerprints all over that final product. You might care about these communities even though you yourself don't live in the neighborhoods, but you don't see them through the eyes of those who do live there, and their view is likely to be very different than yours as an outsider. Fight the tendency to be presumptuous; it is the most respectful position you can take. That's why it's critical to bring in these community grass-tops and grassroots stakeholders: so that your practice can be codesigned with those who will live with the effects of what you create. And *how* you invite them to contribute is as important as the invitation itself.

Look for Those Who've Done Similar Work

When we were looking for allies, we didn't stop at traditional healthcare partner organizations. We looked at nontraditional partners, locally, nationally, and globally. How did we choose them? A lot was based on relationships for us, as it's likely to be for you, because individuals who are like-minded are naturally drawn together. What we looked for was a common thread of service leadership, individuals within organizations who firmly believed and understood that any position of leadership was really just an opportunity to serve a greater number of people in a more impactful way.

BARRY H. OSTROWSKY, RWJBARNABAS HEALTH PRESIDENT AND CEO

There has to be recognition by an organization like ours that there are already people who are driven to help and address these problems. They're typically smaller than we are: they tend to live grant to grant and worry about their financial wherewithal in pursuing their mission. If you just stomp in as the big business, announcing you're going to cure these social ills, that would be a grave mistake. Not only is it insulting to those who have already been endeavoring to help, but you'd be missing on a couple of points. One, unless the community trusts you, this is not going to be successful, and that trust typically is already being extended to some existing nonprofits or mission-driven organizations in the community. And these organizations have preexisting constituencies you want to address as well, so being partners with them is absolutely critical. You're also going to be able to make them more effective, because you could conceivably support them more efficiently in what they do than by building your own infrastructure to deal with the same problems.

We had a preexisting platform of smaller mission-driven, community-based organizations that we met with on a regular basis. When we made the change, we naturally brought it to this group and explained what we wanted to do. They were incredibly excited about it, and we began a planning process with the group to determine what the most pressing and highest-priority social issues were, so that we didn't simply say, "You know what? We think food insecurity is the problem." Or, "Diabetes is the problem." We did it as a group, and they participated in a meaningful way, as partners.

What are we talking about when we're defining traditional and nontraditional healthcare partners? A traditional healthcare partner might be a federally qualified health center (FQHC) or a nonprofit that has a focus on health or wellness. On our community advisory board in the greater Newark area are representatives of the local FQHC and the head of the Maternal Child Health Consortia, for instance. Another traditional policy healthcare partner is the New Jersey Healthcare Quality Institute: they do great research in a number of areas and they have a mayor's wellness campaign. Because they're trying to create a state of health and wellness for communities, they're a logical choice. The Hospital Alliance of New Jersey does great research too, so we might work with them to utilize some of that research toward defining our policy goals and making our case.

A nontraditional partner could be a policy partner like the New Jersey Institute for Social Justice. Though that doesn't sound like a healthcare entity, it was actually their research and partnership that helped us to craft so many of the fundamental elements around our push for local hiring and local procurement opportunities. We also partner with entities that do housing development, like New Jersey Community Capital and the NJ Housing and Mortgage Finance Agency, and many organizations that advocate for community revitalization, like the Housing and Community Development Network of New Jersey or the New Jersey Redevelopment Agency, as well as Hunger Free New Jersey. While all of these are nontraditional healthcare partners, our work and interests overlap and we're aiming for similar goals in trying to create healthier environments and thriving communities.

Nationally, we looked for those who could help us in the space of thought leadership, like the Democracy Collaborative, the Root Cause Coalition, and others. Another national partner was ChangeLab Solutions; while they're based in Oakland, California, they deal with policies, regulations, and laws that create inequitable outcomes and work toward righting them. They take a look across the country at what works and what doesn't, then look at the local environment to figure out how it's most challenged and how best to effectuate the change that needs to happen.

Another nontraditional partner at the national level is United Way. While they're not the kind of organization that a healthcare institution may usually partner with, their national ALICE initiative (asset limited, income constrained, employed) deals with those who make too much to qualify for federal benefits but not quite enough to make ends meet, and we've relied on their terrific research into that group to help us reshape our internal employee policies and frame our external community initiatives. Think Tank, Inc. is another with whom we partnered to develop a healthcare-centered version of their emotionally riveting Cost of Poverty Experience. We engaged clinicians and administrators alike to undergo a month in the life of someone living in poverty. The effort was utilized to raise awareness of the challenge and, indeed, the expense of living under the burden of poverty and trying to navigate the healthcare delivery system. It was eye-opening and highlighted for participants how a lack of understanding and respect for the harsh realities of poverty presented a barrier to achieving health and wellness.

For our global health efforts we partnered with Care One Management, LLC and subsidiary InnovaCare, who were located on the island of Puerto Rico, to help us figure out the logistics of where and how to transport aid to those in need when the island was hit by

Hurricane Maria. We've also partnered with entities like MedShare, a national organization that provides support with medical supplies.

Local partners are critical, because although the work is evidence based and data driven, it also needs to reflect the wishes and needs of the constituents we seek to assist. In order to create a groundswell of support from the community leaders outside of our organization, we talked to those in both commercial and nonprofit enterprises and to the heads of local state and federal governing bodies. As the work is policy led, it's important to have those within the government affairs function directly involved.

That said, it doesn't happen overnight, and patience is required. Trust is something that has to be earned, and when businesses, corporations, or healthcare systems and hospitals begin thinking about doing this work, it's important to realize that trust requires relationship building.

Enlist Your Board Members— and Their Contacts

Your board will likely have people on it who can help, too. Our local community advisory board in the city of Newark, the Greater Newark Advisory Board (GNCAB), has several members of the New Jersey Legislature and city council on it, so when we talk about policies that need to be changed, we have the potential sponsors of legislation sitting at that table. They've been a part of developing our initiatives, so we don't have to orient or educate them about the requisite policy changes that pertain to them. When we first decided to go down this path, we went on a "talking tour" to our statewide legislative and congressional delegations to discuss the issues, how we were thinking of working to address them, and how they could help. Our message to them was, "We're positioning ourselves to make real-life investments in addressing how people work, live, age, worship, and play in our communities for better health outcomes"—not just looking at what sorts of disease they present with.

The SICI practice also relies upon the thought leadership of an external advisory council (EAC). The use of advisory boards to map community-based strategies and social determinants of health assets is a key operational approach for the SICI practice. By working collaboratively across sectors, we are better able to address the social determinants of health positively, thus the practice has called upon several subject-matter experts from across the nation to form the practice's EAC. Members of this interdisciplinary group have expertise in health practices and delivery, housing, population health, social and economic development, business, education, public policy, and philanthropy. The EAC has a guidance/think tank mandate as the SICI team calls upon the EAC members to share their valuable experience and thought leadership in order to further position the SICI practice to make more meaningful and impactful investments in our communities.

Your community, advisory, or corporate board likely has people on it who are well-respected decision makers in their industries, and those contacts can be useful if you're looking to identify potential synergies in industries outside of your own. More, the varied and diverse perspectives can only add to your novel approach. The thought leadership of a member of your corporate board with a background in development can assist your initial endeavors in the housing and healthcare space just as the data collected from emergency room high utilizers is better when layered with the personal stories shared by members of the community.

Check Your Assumptions

No corporate entity has a monopoly on being well educated about anyone else's experience.

> **No corporate entity has a monopoly on being well educated about anyone else's experience.**

A primary reason to bring in outside stakeholders to help shape your work is because you want to evidence a deeper respect for them than they traditionally have been accorded. Too many healthcare institutions that assumed they had great community relations have found themselves embarrassed when it was revealed how neglected their surrounding community felt by them. Don't be that institution.

Expect to face a fair amount of skepticism, even cynicism, about your efforts and your motives—even from those they're designed to help. A South Ward community group in Newark had been doing a lot of great work, but we'd never been invited to be a part of it. One of our team members was raised in the city and still lives there, so they were asked to attend a meeting on our behalf. When they did so, an elderly lady, a community grandmother, who'd been with the group since its beginning didn't hesitate to ask just who they were and what they were doing there: "I have lived in the South Ward my entire life. Who are you?" It sounds harsh, but you have to remember that this beloved community, like so many other urban, underresourced communities across the country, has grown accustomed to being studied, surveyed, and examined without reaping any of the benefits of this scholarly research. It has even suffered from outsiders being self-appointed leaders and parachuting in on them. It is customary to receive a message like, "Don't come here and tell me how I'm living or about my experience, because nobody's a better expert on that than I am," and that is to be deeply respected.

That's why it's important to show a high level of respect and humility. Diana Ortiz-Candelejo, a SICI corporate team member, talked about who she was and who she was representing, but she was met with a lot of "uh-huh" and "mm-hmm" until she said, "I am not from the South Ward, but I am from Newark, the East Ward to be exact. I am a lifelong resident of this city, and I look forward to learning from you." Once she said that, the ice melted a bit, and she was basically told, "Okay, you can sit there and listen for a while"— and she did. Eventually she was asked, "Diana, what do you think? What's your experience?" But she waited until she was asked—and that's critical.

DIANA ORTIZ-CANDELEJO, DIRECTOR, ANCHOR MISSION, SOCIAL IMPACT AND COMMUNITY INVESTMENT TEAM AT RWJBH

Believe it or not, I myself am a beneficiary of RWJBH anchor mission initiatives. When the city of Newark's Newark 2020 initiative was being raised, I was presented to leaders of anchor institutions as a sort of case study for the mayor's office, because I couldn't find employment. I have a master's in public administration from the London School of Economics (LSE). I'm a Newark native who grew up in the city of Newark and went to Newark public schools from pre-K all the way up through high school. I still live in Newark. I had an undergraduate degree in economics from Drew University and that graduate school degree from LSE. But until the Newark 2020 initiative gave the impetus to local hiring by anchor institutions and helped put me in touch with the CEOs of those institutions, I was unemployed. Now, as the director of the community investment team at RWJBH, I oversee the high level of the anchor mission initiative: "hire local, buy local, and invest local." It's a work in progress and one we're still figuring out every day. But I'm living proof that it works.

These groups are accustomed to ivory tower institutions coming in and trying to tell them something about the data or the research, but they're not used to hearing, "Listen, you are the experiential experts here. You tell me: What can we change about our own practice or our process? What can we do differently, so that we're not forcing you to navigate unfamiliar waters? How would you prefer that we interface and engage with you? Does our data match your lived experience or do you think there are other priorities you wish to collaborate on?"

Clearly, this calls for a certain level of social and cultural competence, because being presumptuous about what you know and what you don't, or not being cognizant of your own implicit bias, will be perceived as hugely disrespectful and can damage your brand's reputation. I recall a particular presidential campaign that sent young volunteers into urban, historically African American churches without ever teaching or training them about the rules for respectful engagement in that environment. Eighteen- and twenty-one-year-olds from wealthy suburbs were walking in and calling elderly African American women by their first names. That's a huge no-no! That's not how that works. When we meet someone, it is Ms. Helen, Dona Izabella, etc. until you're told otherwise. Make sure your representatives understand the rules of culturally competent engagement, and if they are multicultural and multifaceted, as they often are, please invest in training for your team. This is an important step. Don't skip it. You can have the best intentions in the world, but if you don't approach people in a culturally competent manner, you won't be welcome.

LOURDES VALDEZ, CORPORATE DIRECTOR OF WORKFORCE DEVELOPMENT AND GRANTS FOR RWJBH

Successful community collaboration requires a lot of communication. It requires humility. You cannot be proud and do this work. You have to be humble and to go in with the attitude of, "I don't know everything, and somebody has something to teach me." You need to have that willingness to learn and hear somebody else's perspective. It's important not to be narrow-minded: you have to drop your barriers. We're humans, and humans come with different barriers, different issues, and you have to be very creative in how you address those issues to remove the barriers. To me, it's about being flexible, persistent, and open minded.

Seek out the elders and those whom your community holds in respect; locate the elderly Latina grandmother who is *the* abuela in her community and invest the time to make her your trust ambassador who will vouch for you to others. Arrogance wins no allies, especially in communities or populations that have not historically been treated respectfully by the powers that have invaded their communities. Too many institutions skip this step at their cost. And don't imagine that simply including them to be polite won't be seen for exactly what it is. For us, being invited to a community meeting in the South Ward was a tremendous breakthrough, because even though Newark Beth

Israel Medical Center has been there for 119 years and the Children's Hospital of New Jersey sits within that hospital, we had never been invited guests to these meetings before.

How Can You Establish Yourself As a Trustworthy Partner?

As a change agent, how can you begin to breach those barriers that have historically kept your organization apart from the community it serves? *Show up*. Start attending some of the community meetings without trying to put yourself or your cause on their agenda. Go to actively listen, to learn before you try to speak. And we're not talking about a one-time appearance; it's a process that will require continuing effort.

Volunteer in the community; meet those who have boots on the ground and are already helping. People need to see that you're sincere, and that's a reasonable expectation. Reach out as an interested party regarding the issues they're concerned with, not as the hero on the white horse riding to the rescue. I'm not talking about sending line staff; I'm talking about sending senior executives to those meetings. At some point, those people you're trying to learn from will let you know that they're ready to have substantive conversations with you, especially if you're showing an active learning kind of attitude: "I want to get a sense of what you're doing and how you're doing it. Is there a way we could assist?"

Leave the ivory tower: go to them, don't expect them to come to you. Go visit their site or their community center, spend time touring it, seeing what they're offering, and show sensitivity to the challenges they're dealing with. Ask thoughtful questions and really listen to the answers. You'll learn things you need to know, and they'll begin to see you're sincere in your interest. One of our best examples of this is Mariam Merced, director of community health promotions, our SICI facility leader at RWJUH in New Brunswick. She's an incredibly valuable member of the greater New Brunswick community and has long volunteered, serving both within and alongside community organizations and investing in trust-building relations.

Connecting with Your Community

How do you connect with the people whose input and buy-in you'll need to bring your community around?

Begin with your municipal leadership: your mayor and your city council members. Your local municipality almost certainly has an economic development corporation or a community development corporation (CDC) of some kind. I don't mean a local chamber of commerce; chambers are associations that are created for the betterment of the businesses that are in it, whereas an economic development corporation is geared toward ushering in economic development and redevelopment. Go to them, because they will help you to better understand the strategy for the city in that space. For instance, our prototype city has a lot of economic development in its downtown corridor. We wanted to pull that out to the residential corridors where people live, because we're interested in health and wellness of people in the community.

And while economic development corporations' focus can be primarily on the health of corporations rather than people, we're fortunate that the Newark organization is interested in both. Economic well-being has been shown to be directly linked to health well-being, and understanding their strategy and where they are in its execution, implementation, and development will inform our view. These entities can also help to connect you with important players, because the truth is there are a million nonprofits. Which ones are potential partners in your change effort?

While the federal government can bring some support to change efforts, they're a lot harder to reach and influence. That said, you're going to want to be sure to reach out to your congressional representatives and speak with them about your interest in change agency in order to usher in policy reform. They too would benefit from being on board sooner rather than later in the process and given the opportunity for partnership. Don't begrudge them the opportunity to codesign policies toward encouraging equity.

Who else are corporate anchor communities talking to? You should be contacting your local colleges and universities. Universities have been embracing anchor missions far longer than healthcare institutions have, in most states. Find out who they've been partnering with and with whom you should be speaking. How have they executed their anchor strategies, and is there any potential for intersectionality with their efforts and yours? Community colleges can be great partners in workforce development curriculum creation as they can be more nimble than four-year institutions.

Vetting Your Potential Partners Is an Important Step

Is the grassroots organization you're looking at viable and thriving or more of an overnight sensation? Do they have a reputation for consistency and stability? How is their standing among community members and funders? Remember, you're not just shaping your strategy or framework, but also your implementation and timeline, because you don't want to rush ahead of your community. You want to be walking in lockstep with them toward a shared goal.

When you're reaching out to groups and individuals in pursuit of their partnership and support, it's important to understand their specific missions and what matters to them—and to frame your mission in a way that accords with their focus. A group that's concerned with child welfare may not initially see jobs as part of their mission, unless you can use your data to paint a picture for them of how joblessness in the community impacts vulnerable children. We've learned, for instance, that one of the greatest obstacles faced by children in the community in terms of success in school is the fact that they are so transient. A local principal we met with told us that her school turns over by a third every year—sometimes by midyear—so it's tough to keep track of students and keep them on track academically. Of course, children don't move on their own; their families move because they're housing insecure. Usually their families are housing insecure because their parents are job insecure. And if they're housing and job insecure, they're more than likely to also be food insecure.

As you search for local stakeholders, make sure you're talking to your schools and your public health officer and the health department; you need to know their views of conditions on the ground. We used a documentary we'd produced on food security, *Food for Thought: The Path to Food Security in Newark*, as a way to open a dialogue with many of community stakeholders, grassroots organizations, urban farmers, urban agriculturalists, and residents in Newark. We screened it for clergy, community groups, and others to get their thoughts and input. We went to neighborhood associations and senior associations and asked to have the opportunity to share the film and get their feedback. We showed it to our residents and fellows too, in order to get their thoughts.

KIM COOK, DIRECTOR OF SOCIAL IMPACT AND COMMUNITY INVESTMENT, NEWARK BETH ISRAEL MEDICAL CENTER AND THE CHILDREN'S HOSPITAL OF NEW JERSEY

Our first project was a documentary, which was a pretty ambitious start. It focused on food security in Newark, because Newark is considered a food desert. We used youths from the community, high school students and a couple of middle school children, as citizen journalists. They interviewed people in the community and other stakeholders about food security, and those interviews, comments, and observations were put together as a documentary. Our rationale for using these young people was multipronged: these are kids we're hoping to develop as future leaders, so we wanted to get them engaged with civic activities and encourage them to be concerned about their community and their future.

The film was very powerful. We had an internationally recognized documentary filmmaker on board to edit and put the film together. We had a screening in downtown Newark where we invited members of the community to see it. Since then, we've been traveling around the city in different wards to screen it. We have an hour-long version as well as a twenty-minute version that we take on the road [to facilitate community discussions]. It helps us get people involved and talking, answering questions about their community's needs and what they'd like to see done to address them. As an outcome of that effort, we're now

> taking it to the next step, looking at developing food hubs in each ward since access to healthy food is an issue. We're engaging with the local communities in the different wards around developing food hubs, so that people will have access to healthy food in their area.

Are you talking to your local clergy? You should be in touch with the local association of clergy, because they know what the folks who sit in their pews come to them for help with, and they can help spread the word about your work.

Manage expectations early and often; the fact is, when you—as a representative of this big entity—come calling, some of these folks are going to be expecting that you come bearing a big check. Make it clear why you're there, that you want to learn from them and that you're hoping to address some of their greatest challenges together.

And be sure that the people you're connecting with are also connecting with each other, because networking is good for everyone. Oftentimes, we don't have the answers. But you know who does? Somebody else in the room. These folks may already know each other, but your change effort might help them connect in a way they hadn't before. Sometimes, even though they're in the same community, they don't know each other at all, so the opportunities you present for them to get together and share their goals and challenges help to create many opportunities for trust and collaboration. That way, someone who walks in with a problem, issue, or challenge usually walks out with an answer—and not usually one that comes from us.

JOSEPH SCOTT, EXECUTIVE VICE PRESIDENT FOR HEALTH CARE TRANSFORMATION, RWJBARNABAS HEALTH

How do you make sure you're giving the community what they need? I think the best way to answer that is with an example. In Jersey City, we have a violence problem as our social impact initiative; we were seeing a lot of gunshot wounds at our trauma center, and violence was the number-one issue identified in our community health needs assessment. We set out to work with community groups to identify what the issues were around violence. But rather than dictate what needed to happen, we brought together members of the community to talk about what it means to have violence in their community.

Anchoring your institution and what the community says they need is vitally important—then act on it by being a facilitator, not a dictator, to figure out how you can make things better around a particular issue, to help drive and improve the overall well-being of the community. That's the anchor mission as I see it, and I think that's how it becomes most effective.

That said, one of the potential pitfalls you have to be acutely aware of is, What is the agenda of the people coming to the table? Some of the time, it's about their personal issues rather than what's best for the community, so you have to be very careful in choosing your partners. If somebody is coming to the table to offer a service, is it for their benefit or does it really help the community?

We found ourselves in a situation like that when we were working with a high school in an underserved area, one in which a lot of the students had social and behavioral issues. We put a counseling center there as part of our behavioral health program. It wound up being very effective and a great thing for the students, but initially I had a couple of organizations approach me about being a part of it, and I could tell it was more about giving them money than it was about providing service to those kids. I actually had to turn them down. It created a bit of havoc, because they were politically connected—but we were always steadfast in setting the standard that if we're going to engage someone in a project or process, it has got to be with the primary aim of helping these underserved and vulnerable communities.

GUIDELINES FOR CHANGE AGENTS

- When you're working with external stakeholders, make sure you're doing exactly that—working *with* them, not against them by advancing your sole agenda, and working at their pace, not yours. It's more important to be in step with each other than it is to lead the way.

- Be accountable for what you do—and that includes errors you'll make along the way. If something isn't proceeding in the way you thought it was going to, and it's a problem, be straightforward with them. Don't try to cover anything up; evidence the breakdown, tell them you need to try it again, or in a different way, and get their input.

- Make sure your outside stakeholders get to see the end result of any project or part of a project on which you've asked them to offer their input. Anything less is disrespectful and will be seen as such. An example is the documentary on food insecurity we talked about earlier in the chapter: rather than starting out telling the people in the community what they needed per the data, we took it to the members and representatives of the community on the advisory board and asked them to take it back to their constituents to help us figure out what they thought were the issues to address. Eight months later when the documentary was done, we were able to go back to them and say, "Okay, you said that you wanted the voices of youth involved, so we trained students to be journalists. You said that you wanted to make certain we talked to them about systems and structural change; not just how to plant and grow some produce, but historic inequity and the disparate impact that caused their community to lack easy access to affordable, nutritious, organic produce, so we've paired them with PhD students from the New Jersey Institute of Technology who taught them about food distribution chains as well as the distribution systems and the history of their origins." We wanted to make sure they saw that they were asked, heard, and listened to, that their desires and experiences were significantly infused into the project.

- Within historically disenfranchised communities, people are tired of being studied like subjects. If part of what you're doing requires a survey or survey data, try to collaborate with other community-based organizations or municipalities to draw from other similar surveys, so people aren't pestered with unnecessary phone calls or people knocking at their doors.

It's especially galling to those who feel that the researchers are coming from privileged backgrounds and looking at those they're surveying as subjects. This is an opportunity for coeducation; behave accordingly.

CHAPTER FIVE

Getting Your Board on Board

One big hurdle that you as a change agent need to clear is getting your board of directors to back your efforts and give your plan their seal of approval and support. Depending on the makeup of your board, both in terms of the demographics and the personalities involved, this can be challenging.

Those who are traditionalists in the healthcare delivery hospital industry may find it quite difficult to understand what it is you're talking about and how it applies to what they see as your organization's core business. Why in the world would a hospital consider getting into the business of creating housing or growing food? But, of course, if as an organization our primary concern is health, then it's logical to consider all the factors impacting the wellness of those you serve. Still, in this situation we were pitching a program that from the board's point of view had not previously existed, so we knew going in that we had to be prepared for justifiable resistance.

In our case, exhaustive research and CEO commitment were both tremendously necessary in building our case for change to our board. Being attorneys by background and training, we were both quite familiar with the need for establishing proofs at trial, and in this circumstance, we worked to approach our board with that same kind of thoroughness and advance planning. After all, they didn't know how we'd come to this plan or what influenced us in our journey, and we needed to be able to help them to see what we saw in the data.

Our summation, we decided, would be painting the picture of a more equitable future that we as an institution could help to create, one in which everyone has a chance to grow up healthy and strong, and one where there were no longer pockets of the powerless who wound up suffering poor health outcomes.

Preparation Is Critical

In preparing for this "do or die" effort, the CEO set aside generous swathes of his valuable time, four hours at a stretch, where we and our advisors in this space would put on our waders and get into the cranberry bogs of data we'd amassed: the intervention strategies that others had employed, the unique nuances of our local communities, as well as best practices endorsed by the CDC and the World Health Organization. As excited as we both were about the effort, this was really Barry's vision. We built the evidence around the intervention strategies that research and data had proven effective in impacting these social determinants of health so that our board—our jury—would feel brought in to the journey.

The challenge for the change agent is to create a compelling narrative, one that simultaneously engages the listener and invites them to join the effort, without overwhelming them with the size or complexity of the task. That's why we walked them through the utilization and presentation of evidence-based and evidence-informed research—so our listeners understood that this wasn't sending money into a black hole, but was in fact an investment, not a donation.

Our board was not atypical, demographically, of the kinds of people you generally find involved at this level in large nonprofits. As is customary, each of them is at the top of their respective fields, well respected and well reputed—again, typical board members for an organization of this size. As businesspeople, and in some cases attorneys themselves, they bring business savvy and legal acumen that serves the organization exceptionally well. They are also incredibly dedicated to the institution and they get along well with each other.

At the point of launch of the SICI, we had a brand-new board that had just come together as a result of the largest merger in healthcare history in the state. That meant half the board members weren't nearly as familiar to us as those with whom we had worked for years. We couldn't have predicted that some of these new board members, including the new board chair, would take our mission to heart and become its biggest champions.

These individuals range from shrewd businesspersons to commercial real estate developers, physicians, and top academicians. But this mission hit them square in the hearts and heads as they understood the opportunity of both upstream prevention and downstream treatment.

BARRY OSTROWSKY, PRESIDENT AND CEO, RWJBARNABAS HEALTH

An effort like this has to begin with the mission objective. I think it's very difficult to defend something outside the more or less conventional clinical platform that is going to use resources but not give you financial return, unless it's linked directly to a mission objective. That's why this effort first required the board to accept an alteration in our mission, which was to move to health, defined as showing improvement in the community's overall health. Then, it's a matter of, "What plans do you have to execute toward that mission?" When you explain that these social determinants can be addressed in programs that do require resources, and that the positive impact will be seen in the lives of people over probably generations, then I think you build the context within which you can defend and certainly justify that allocation of resources without a financial return, necessarily.

Delivering the Pitch

The pitch itself was planned for the very first board retreat for this newly formed entity, and SICI was to be the closing session at this two-day event.

The night before, a talk on the policy and political lay of the land was presented, and television political pundits and strategists were brought in to discuss healthcare delivery generally and the landscape in New Jersey specifically. The following day, members of the senior management team provided presentations in their specialty areas; for instance, the chief medical officer gave a presentation about patient safety and quality clinical care and the chief financial officer did a presentation about the financial well-being of the institution. Ours was the very last one; we delivered it with PowerPoint illustrations, videos, and partner speakers and even wheeled in a bed of produce we'd grown in our hydroponic greenhouse, with big pictures of school children learning how to grow fresh fruit and vegetables, to make certain they saw this in real time. We knew that we had to make it something tangible, something they could feel, access, and understand, so everyone got a little gift bag of some of that greenhouse-grown produce to take home.

Because collective impact is so critical to the success of the work, we brought in one of our partner collaborators from Rutgers University, Dr. Kevin Lyons, the assistant dean of supply chain. As a big part of our urban agricultural initiative is around increasing the community's access to fresh produce, we wanted to make it clear how that partnership would enhance and enrich our efforts.

Along with the diversity of the presentation and the input from our invited guest, we wanted to give the board members real-time, real-life examples about the challenges that existed in the towns where our hospitals are located. We passed out maps of the South Ward of Newark that showed a section of town with the locations of three tiny food stores—bodegas, corner stores, and gas stations—that were the only sources of food in the area. Illustrating that helped them to better understand the challenges people in our community face to get food—much less healthy, fresh, nutritious produce. It was eye-opening and really got them engaged on a meaningful level with the "why" of the effort.

There are a lot of ways that getting your board engaged can potentially go wrong, and many of them center on your presentation. You don't want to put people on the defensive; you don't want to shame them or to make them feel as though you're asking for (or demanding) charity. We knew when the board began asking the kinds of great questions that showed they were really looking at this in a serious, practical way that we were winning them over. But we didn't discover how engaged the new board chair, Jack Morris, was until much later, after Hurricane Maria had devastated Puerto Rico. An aspect of this work is global health, and the chair inquired about our medical and health relief efforts in response to the hurricane. The chair wanted to know what, if anything, we were considering, and when told, his response was, "Michellene, I'd actually like to offer you the use of my planes, and to go with you, if you're planning to take aid there."

He followed through on his promise and, along with no fewer than twelve physicians, we visited the main trauma center of the Caribbean and met with the secretary of health of Puerto Rico. It really underlined how aligned our values were and evidenced that our then-chairman had a heart for this kind of work.

If you're confidently imagining that everyone who hears your pitch will be moved to jump on board, it's probably wiser to temper your optimism. While it's likely some of your board members will get it, there will be others whose backgrounds, predispositions, or frames of reference may make them harder to enlist.

There are all kinds of dynamics in play anytime you get a group of people together to make decisions, and you can't hope to understand them all going in. The best you can do as a change maker is to keep your eye on your true north and just keep moving toward it. Don't let yourself be drawn into the back and forth, the politics, or the jockeying for position. It's a distraction, and you just can't do it. You can get lost in the weeds, and that serves nobody. So many people are driven by a fear of scarcity, and that dictates their initial negative response to any pull on shared resources. Adopting an anchor mission requires that you feel that the universe provides abundantly and that there is plenty to go around, so there's no need for sharp elbows. Things work better for all of us when we're working together to accomplish our goals.

A deep commitment to community investment requires us to be ambassadors of the light and know that we are here in order to truly make the world a better place. Some folks are going to throw mud at you.

> **Things work better for all of us when we're working together to accomplish our goals.**

Do we get into the playpen with them and roll around in the mud, or do we just keep moving toward the light? It's a choice we each have to make as we go along. Once we've made that choice, and even if there's occasionally a rock mixed in with that mud they're throwing, we have to refuse to engage on that level. That brings a certain level of integrity to the work and gives credibility to the intentionality of the work. And while we are not here to hurt or harm anyone, doing this work will mean that we have to call out certain things at certain times, because that's what change agents are and that's what we do. Keep your head up, tell the truth, and keep moving forward.

Make the Business Case

How can a change agent who may not have been a litigator effectively present his or her case to a board? The most powerful case you can make to your board is the business case, because most if not all of them are likely to share and appreciate a business plan frame of reference. In our case, we could talk about things like readmission rates and what they were costing us. What could we do to change that? What were the prototypes or pilots we'd seen across the country that have successfully addressed the problem that's causing the institution to lose money? If you can connect that back to the work you want to see done, you're making a compelling business case.

The most important thing is to remember what's important to your audience and to speak their language. Our board is populated with many individuals who have been extremely successful in business, and that's their world, so we made a point to make the business case for the work as convincingly as we made the social case. Know something—know a lot—about the audience you're going to be advocating to and speak *to* them, not *at* them. I know what's important to me, but in order to convince you, I need to present it in terms that are important to you.

We had a variety of backgrounds of the people on our board—several large commercial real estate developers, entrepreneurs, and individuals that came from academia. We made sure that our pitch was made in language common to all of them. We talked about the cost of healthcare to the GDP and about the way in which those costs were only rising, while our health outcomes were not. While some healthcare outcomes were actually getting better, the racial disparity of those outcomes was also widening, and simply letting that continue was not going to support a healthier, more equitable society. We talked about the workers required on any large commercial project and about the need to have a workforce that is healthy enough to come back every day. We talked about the communities we work in and how, when we hire locally, we are giving that entire community an economic stimulus. It's a little bit different when the person lives elsewhere but then comes to work on that particular project, because the paycheck you give them goes right back to where they live but not to the community where they work—the community that gave them the paycheck.

For the entrepreneurs and corporate CEOs, we pointed to the Edelman Trust Barometer and consumer loyalty and what our customer/client base is looking for from healthcare in particular. Consumers expect all companies to do a certain amount of what is referred to as social responsibility work, but they expect healthcare to do much more of it, at a higher rate, in a more sustainable manner, and for a significantly longer period of investment. Consumers today are aware of the records of philanthropy that both for-profit and nonprofit entities have, and that's why they'll bypass their local supermarket to drive out to a place that sells sustainable coffee beans; they want to feel that their choice contributes to positive change, even if the cost is greater to them. Didn't we want and need to be their hospital of choice, the one they associate with that kind of effort, without needing to make any cost greater?

Some members of our board had important backgrounds in policy, so having this work be policy-driven made all the sense in the world to them. In framing your presentation, it's politic to cite studies your board members' corporate, philanthropic, or policy entities have published. Should you have members in finance or associated with banks, include that institution's work on how banks comply with the Community Reinvestment Act, which was created to encourage commercial banks to help meet borrowers' needs, including those in low-income and moderate-income communities.

This isn't about shifting your mission focus to reflect your listeners as much as it is about helping people to see themselves in the work you're outlining, because you're asking them to go on a journey, and that can feel risky. People don't like risk, generally, but if you can help them see that "hmm, I may not know this journey, but I recognize this vehicle," you make it a lot easier for them to get climb aboard and join you on the journey. But there is risk, and it's important to acknowledge that up front; in fact, we'd say...

Don't Shy Away from the Element of the Risk—Take It on, Head-on

One way to defuse the kind of resistance that could potentially derail your effort is to address your board's or top leadership's worries first—before anyone else has time to bring them up. Do not hide from the issue of risk in trying to do this work; don't let them have to ask a question that you should have anticipated. Put it up front, literally. In our opening remarks we said, "This is a nontraditional role for a healthcare institution to take, but we will not be the first healthcare institution that has chosen to take it." We had the facts, figures, and names of others to present, and we spoke to them about the leaders in this space—Kaiser Permanente, ProMedica, and Gundersen, among others—and pointed out, "We can choose to stay on the safe side, of course—with all the others whose names nobody knows." We talked about the advantage of evaluating and taking *smart risk*; not uncalculated or blind risk, but thoughtful, deliberate, and well-researched risk. We warned them to expect resistance—and to be ready to push through it.

BARRY H. OSTROWSKY, PRESIDENT AND CEO, RWJBARNABAS HEALTH

When we presented our case for this work to the board, there really was more or less immediate recognition, based on the data, that what we were doing already was not sufficient. For the most part, we deal with vulnerable urban communities in New Jersey, and if you put up the data about disproportionate illness and disproportionately challenging conditions of people living in those communities, sadly, the need speaks for itself.

While there was no questioning that the data we presented was accurate in reflecting those realities, there were questions around: "How are you going to determine actual resource allocation?" and "While we don't expect a return on investment, how are you going to evaluate success when you roll out projects?" They didn't expect us to have the answers for those questions at that moment; to some extent, we had preempted that by saying we would have budgets and programs and that we would have metrics to show whether or not we were making progress. I think they were satisfied with that, and they've become even greater champions of this as time has gone on. That said, unless you as a change agent are prepared to put forward a pretty strong factual or even semiacademic platform to your board on why they should buy in on this, I don't think you can expect to get very far. I mean, this is a six-billion-dollar company, and you can't be chasing a whim. You have to be able to say, "This is the real data. This is the reality. We either want to address it or not."

In fact, I gave the board members that option: I said, "Look, this is what your management team would like to do. If, for whatever reasons, you feel that it's not appropriate, we can continue to do our conventional work. I just want everyone to realize that no matter how effective we are in that regard, we will still have communities that we think will be disproportionately suffering, but that's not to suggest it shouldn't be taken up by somebody else." They didn't like that option, as of course we didn't, and so we got their blessing to go the route we're on.

It's important, too, to frame the ongoing efforts in that way as we continue to meet and discuss the work and its progress. I remind the board at every board meeting of what our mission is. They need to hear it said, and it doesn't have to be empha- sized any more strongly than simply to say, "In our pursuit of our mission to make our communities healthier, the following is being done." I think reinforcement of this idea is critically important, because if it's not reiterated, it's very easy to default to patting ourselves on the backs because we just did our eighty-second heart transplant, or something like that.

When you open with this kind of honesty, you're making it tougher to shoot holes in your proposal—and you're giving those board members who are inclined to take the journey with you an easier on-ramp.

GUIDELINES FOR CHANGE AGENTS

- Just as you've done your due diligence in preparing your facts and marshaling your figures, you're going to have to put the same amount of thought, care, and research into shaping your presentation to resonate with the audience to whom you're speaking. Don't rely solely on facts and figures to do the trick. You have to speak their values language and cast your efforts in terms they can appreciate.

- The key here is research. You may or may not know your board members, but either way, you need to know them better if you want to earn their buy-in. What field is the board member in, and in what position? What kind of commitment to corporate social responsibility does that company have? Are they or their company particularly philanthropic? If so, to what kinds of causes? Explore their entities' giving history, read up on what they've done, and think through how what you're proposing relates to them.

- Don't waste their time. These people donate their work on the board to your institution, and their time is valuable. Make certain they understand that their presence and their contribution is seen and appreciated by you.

- Don't talk down to them. You may be the expert in your space, but chances are that they're the experts in theirs. Watch your tone, and don't condescend. You're not teaching a roomful of students, or even necessarily telling them what they don't know. This is an invitation you're issuing, not a homework assignment.

- Know your data cold, and use it to enlighten them, not as a cudgel to hit them with. If someone has a preconceived idea that doesn't reflect the facts, be gentle in sharing that. Again, your goal is buy-in.

- Speak their language; explaining this work from a legal affairs lens would not necessarily help to get a CFO on board. You have to see it through his or her lens. What challenges are each of them likely to see, and how does your change effort address or potentially mitigate those? Find the intersectionality.

CHAPTER SIX

Everything Is Local

I n a big enterprise or organization with multiple locations in differing communities, your mandate will need modification in order to best serve local needs. How do you apply this mandate? Not just to your entity as a corporate system, but what does it look like when it's localized in each of your facilities and the communities in which they sit?

Clearly your efforts have to be based on and reflective of the needs of that particular community. Narrowing that down can be challenging, but it's crucial to your success that you be specific in your goals. To do so, you'll need input from those living in the community and also the overview that demographic data on the community can provide. And to accomplish those goals once you've clarified them, you'll need input and partnerships—with community resident members, both appointed and community-anointed leaders, and businesses.

BARRY H. OSTROWSKY, PRESIDENT AND CEO, RWJBARNABAS HEALTH

We had a preexisting platform of smaller mission-driven community-based organizations that we met with on a regular basis. When we made this change in our mission, we of course brought it to this group and explained what we wanted to do. They were incredibly excited about it, and we began a planning process with this group to determine what the most pressing and highest-priority social issues were so that we didn't simply say, "You know what? We think food insecurity is the problem" or "Diabetes is the problem." We did it as a group with them, and they participated in a meaningful way, and so we are, importantly, partners with them as we do this.

On the other side, particularly in a city like Newark, there are big corporate interests, like Prudential, and the big utilities, all of whom over the years have tried to address some of these things or at least provide some support for those who were addressing them, but not in a concerted and perhaps not in a particularly effective way. I spoke to the CEOs of those organizations and said, "Look, as far as I'm concerned, this is our core business. We'd love you to help. We understand it's not your core business, but if, for instance, chronic unemployment is a very big issue, and together we want to be able to hire people from the community who unfortunately are chronically unemployed, perhaps undertrained, we need programs to do that," and they willingly signed on for that.

I think if you make partnerships with other business interests whose core businesses are not this in particular, and you engage in a meaningful and humble way with community-based organizations that have been endeavoring to make life better for people for decades, then you start to build the kind of partnerships that are effective. Failure to work with the latter, namely the small, community-focused organizations, will in fact, in my view, make success impossible.

In our case, our Newark location is addressing food insecurity, while our Somerset location is dealing with transitional housing; our Jersey City location is addressing violence, and our New Brunswick location is addressing both housing and violence. Why? Because our focus was on making a substantial, sustainable, actual impact in the communities, and doing so in a way that reflects the most pressing needs of each. What informed our choices was the community-specific data gleaned from a variety of sources. Our hospitals conducted community health needs assessments, which were informed by community partners and shared with the community boards of each location for their vetting and verification. Did our results mirror the reality of what was being felt in local neighborhoods? Did identified needs reflect daily challenges of residents and organizations working in a particular community? The only way to know was to engage the community.

The Community Advisory Board

Creating a dynamic and functioning community advisory board is critical to your success, not only in how you shape and focus your work, but in conveying it to the people you're trying to assist. Your community board should include both grass-tops and grassroots, elected leaders and local residents, law enforcement, K-12 and higher education, of course, and the head of the clergy association, but also those who run *and* use community-based organizations, because you want to make certain that you are in some way tapping into the experience of residents of the community. Why? In our experience, the process of getting information indirectly from them to us can resemble the telephone game we all played in elementary school, in that the facts of the story change, the nuance of first-person experience gets lost, and implicit bias can easily get applied in the retelling of the story as it gets passed from one person to the next. In order for you to have a good sense of the reality on the ground, and, quite frankly, for you to be as respectful as possible through an asset-based rather than a deficient-based lens, you want to make sure you are running the data you've received through those who are the experts of their experience. While we give a lot of credit to folks who walk in with advanced degrees, what also matters is the input of individuals who live the experience of struggle, who live the experience of poverty, of being in a particular community day to day, and giving them a great deal of authority to define their own destiny. Living with dignity should not be a luxury reserved only for some.

> **Living with dignity should not be a luxury reserved only for some.**

In our case, our community health needs assessments told us what diseases or conditions were most prevalent in the patient community served; for example, heart disease and asthma. What could be causing the high rate of pediatric asthma patients we're seeing? When you take a step back and look at it through the eyes of a person who lives there, you'll learn something such as "That's because our community has the cement plant, the county incinerator, and the recycling plant, while neighboring suburban neighborhoods have none. Historical systems have contributed to locating these types of plants within urban, low-income communities. This isn't happenstance," and you realize you're not going to get to the root of this issue via nebulizer and additional treatments for asthma, because it's not going to change in any substantive way until you address the underlying environmental issues.

As our program at Robert Wood Johnson University Hospital in New Brunswick has shown, health of the family can be immediately affected by addressing the negative environmental factors within the home. With their New Brunswick Healthy Homes Collaborative initiative, they're visiting homes with ambassadors from the community that folks can trust to say, "Listen, let me take a look at what's going on here, so that we can try to help ameliorate some of the health issues you're presenting with." What we're finding is that a variety of situations often boil down to whether you have a good or a bad landlord. If the upstairs apartment has been leaking water into your apartment, and mold is growing in the walls of the nursery where your child sleeps, chronic asthma issues are an outcome of that. In other areas, the challenge is infestations, because when folks live in high population density with low economic resources in close proximity to industrial areas and in nontraditional residential areas, rodents will flourish. We're going into homes and trying to help folks to deal with it, trying to make certain we are working collaboratively in order to ameliorate it, because if an individual in one apartment deals with something, but the family two units down hasn't dealt with it, the problem will return.

MARIAM MERCED, DIRECTOR OF COMMUNITY HEALTH PROMOTIONS, ROBERT WOOD JOHNSON UNIVERSITY HOSPITAL

We were fortunate to partner with other community-based organizations to do this Healthy Homes project and to be part of a grant from the Robert Wood Johnson Foundation that the hospital matched. New Brunswick has a blueprint for health (also grant funded by the Robert Wood Johnson Foundation), and housing was one of the big issues within that blueprint. Our community health improvement plan and our community health needs assessment had flagged multiple issues related to housing. Housing is always one of those big things that comes up in our assessments, along with transportation, medical issues, and asthma. So, when we put all of that together, we looked for a project that could address all those needs and also could be our social impact project.

Through that grant funding, we hired a program coordinator, then identified six community health promoters, women that were Spanish speaking and who were trusted in the community. Many of them already had training as community health promoters, because they'd worked on a couple of other projects in the city around diabetes and beautification. We trained them in the seven principles of healthy homes, then sent them out in pairs to visit homes with a questionnaire. The homes were assessed for mold and pest infestation, whether anyone smoked in the home, and whether the smoke detectors were working; all of those kinds of things. This year we're following up on the issues we found and making recommendations to the city about what we think needs to be done. Out of that effort, the department of health has started checking everybody that goes through their clinic for lead, and the office of rent control is now going to be posting landlords' names and addresses so people can go there and find information about an apartment they want to rent.

Using these community health promoters created the bridge that let us be invited into peoples' homes. We are in a very difficult time with the current administration, in that they've stepped up prosecution of immigrants, and many in the community are afraid of ICE. But these ladies were familiar to their community and understood their problems at a personal level, so they had a real passion to do this kind of work. The first time I went out with the team, we went to visit the home of a young Latina family, a mother and father and a couple of kids. The apartment was very well-kept, I must say; we looked at the fire extinguisher and at the smoke detectors. They'd been there eight years; the mother shared that she has asthma, and one child is a hemo-philiac, and she just happened to add, "We have been without heat for a year." It had been a terribly cold winter. She had told the landlord the heat was out a couple of times but had never put anything in writing or saved her texts, so when we tried to go with her to city hall, she didn't have any proof.

Subsequently, we've creating a package that will help people like her to keep that kind of supporting information organized:

their bills, the lists of problems, and photos they've taken. We're helping them to set up Gmail accounts so they can save their pictures and texts, because we saw the need right there. She had a great case, but no proof. She had had no heat for a whole year, because the landlord had told her, "It's too expensive. I'm not fixing that again." When people are undocumented, those landlords can look for any excuse to get them out.

One thing of which we're always mindful is, How can we deal with these issues as a community so we're making certain that no one feels shamed? Critical to that is dealing with it as a public health issue, rather than a personal family issue. Many people are working two and three jobs just to keep food on the table; what most of us think of as necessities are, for them, luxuries. They don't need to be made to feel ashamed about having to live in unhealthy environments they didn't create and can't mitigate alone.

Communities in which residents have more resources and pay higher taxes are more likely to be heard when they raise complaints about local conditions—but in fact, every community contains vulnerable populations facing various challenges. Somerset is, for instance, a fairly well-resourced suburban area, but it's been hit very hard by the opioid crisis sweeping America. Addiction, like domestic violence, doesn't have just one victim; it impacts the entire family. We saw there were issues around housing related to this; for instance, the need for transitional housing for families who have become housing insecure due to medical costs and are further exploring sober living facilities where individuals who are trying to beat their addictions can go to live, away from the environment where they got addicted in the first place.

As you fine-tune your anchor mission work, be sure you're properly addressing your community's needs in a culturally competent manner, as defined by the people in the community who will be impacted.

What kind of diversity of representatives makes for an effective and useful advisory board? We've talked quite a lot about our work in Newark, and since the community advisory board there is so well formed and effective, let's use it as an example.

Local government is represented by the president of the city council; there are also representatives from state government, the senator and the two assemblypersons from two of the districts that serve the city. That's beneficial to other members in that it provides an avenue of access to policy makers for those from community-based organizations who might not have access easily, because as a general rule the legislators aren't sending staff members to the meetings but are attending the meetings themselves.

We have the county sheriff as the representative of law enforcement. We have clergy represented by a minister who has a church in the ward of the city where our hospital sits, who's also the leader of the community clergy association. The head nurse for the school district serves on the board, providing insight on what she's seeing regarding student health at our local schools. We have a representative from our local unions, who also represents small business within the community. We also have members who represent community organizations threaded throughout the city in different wards.

One, for example, is the Ironbound Community Corporation, which is a comprehensive community-based organization that provides childcare, adult education, early childhood education, and community planning. Among other services, they feed between two hundred and four hundred families in the section of the city where they exist. And while their committed CEO holds the seat, he often sends designees who work most closely with these families, who bring us their concerns so we get more of that insight into the room and at the table. Another community partner, Babyland Family Services, provides daycare, has a beautiful shelter for women fleeing domestic violence, and provides families in need with everything from clothes to baby essentials. These are all significant community-based organizations. From them, we get the chance to hear directly from those they serve.

Of course, we also have traditional healthcare partners at the table: the largest federally qualified health center in the city and the official who heads the city's department of health. We have public health officials from neighboring towns as well, because we understand that people don't live in boxes, and if Newark has an issue, then Irvington or Hillside, two and four miles away, respectively, are likely to have one too. We have the South Ward Children's Alliance and the leader of the Business Improvement District so that the voices of parents and of the business community are also heard.

We are also extremely fortunate in our Newark Community Advisory Board to have a very strong facilitator and friend, Dr. Steve Adubato, professional broadcaster, former NJ state assemblyman, and native Newark resident, who keeps us on track and probes the group to ensure we are asking ourselves the tough questions. While you do not need a professional moderator, it is recommended to have a strong facilitator who can be a timekeeper, moderate, and ensure that everyone's voice is heard.

GRASS-TOPS AND GRASSROOTS

We formed our advisory board as we did because we wanted it to mirror our society. Our institution, like most healthcare institutions, does not necessarily reflect the faces of our diverse society. This group provides an intersectional lens that lets us look at our community through a kaleidoscope of needs, assets, challenges, and opportunities so that as we address a policy topic, an initiative, or a goal, we are getting meaningful and varied input. Together, the group looked at the health challenges of our community, specifically heart disease, hypertension, and diabetes, and realized that most of them were tied to poor eating and childhood and adult obesity—so providing community education and access to nutritious fresh produce and addressing food insecurity became the mission.

When we identified that our mission in Somerset would include providing transitional housing for families who were dealing with housing insecurity as a result of chronic illness, it was determined through a similar collaborative of stakeholders within the community. With that housing available, families could stay together as they tried to heal, because for many, one illness, one injury, or one job loss can wind up putting an entire family on the streets.

It's really important to note that every facility was at a different stage in the creation of their community advisory boards. None of this got rolled out immediately, because it is incredibly important that you not go faster than your community is ready for. So, for some of our facilities, their initial social impact initiative was, literally, working to create a community advisory board because they did not have a preexisting one. Our communities have been speaking to us for decades, but in the corporate space, oftentimes because they don't attempt to communicate to us in the language we have designed, we act as if they aren't speaking at all, and that simply is not true. We need to be flexible and begin to understand and appreciate that they have the right to speak to us in their language, not ours; we need to be better attuned in order to translate these needs.

DARRELL TERRY, PRESIDENT AND CEO, NEWARK BETH ISRAEL MEDICAL CENTER AND CHILDREN'S HOSPITAL OF NEW JERSEY

We're starting to understand the importance of involving the community in the conceptual phase all the way through the implementation phase, as opposed to just creating things that we think are good for people. It's made it more of a conversation. We're not telling you, as a community member, what you need: we're having a dialogue about what's needed and how we might be able to help. You're telling us what your needs are and the barriers, concerns, and issues. There are a bunch of unintended consequences to almost every decision we make. However, if we communicate effectively and involve people, then we can avoid some of those unintended consequences.

Look Outside the Box for Corporate Partners

While partnerships for anchor collaboratives have typically been "eds and meds"—universities and hospitals—the other two hospitals in the city weren't in a position to be able to engage at the time that we were ready to launch. Many standalone hospitals find it hard enough to try and stay financially solvent, so their leadership doesn't always understand the rationale of the work against the competing interest of lowered reimbursement and cash on hand, and that the conditions it addresses have measurable, significant impacts on health outcomes. If you can't get buy-in from traditional anchor players, remember that you're a change agent and you need to be nimble, so look elsewhere. That's how we wound up partnering with corporate entities that are nontraditional anchors.

We were very fortunate in our work in Newark that there are many large corporate entities with which to partner. Many of the corporate institutions headquartered in Newark have partnered to form the Newark Anchor Collaborative (NAC). NAC has adopted a set of shared principles to build a community of practice to support equitable growth in Newark, particularly through the hire, buy, live local strategies. RWJBH was one of the founding institutions along with Audible, New Jersey Institute of Technology, New Jersey Performing Arts Center, Prudential, Rutgers University–Newark, and Rutgers Biomedical and Health Sciences. Since its formation, the network has expanded to include PSE&G, Panasonic, and Broadridge Financial Solutions and is growing.

The NAC is governed by an advisory committee managed by the Newark Alliance. The Newark Alliance is responsible for executing the vision of the advisory committee and acts as a liaison between the NAC and Mayor Ras Baraka's Newark2020 Initiative. The NAC quarterly meetings are cochaired by the NAC board chair, Chancellor Nancy Cantor of Rutgers University–Newark, who is a nationally recognized expert in anchor work, and Aisha Glover, CEO of the Newark Alliance. The added benefit of having a direct connection to the mayor's vision via Newark2020 and the Newark Alliance is that it provided necessary leverage to get CEOs at the table as hire and buy local initiatives were in their infancy.

Prudential provides support for the structure of the NAC, which is incredibly important for any collaborative to operate with effectiveness. Prudential has also provided support for the buy local strategy by hosting meetings of NAC member procurement officers and hosting Local Vendor summits. The Local Vendor summit provided

NAC anchors an opportunity to meet Newark vendors that were recommended by their peer anchors. Identifying and vetting local and diverse businesses can be a challenge but this was one approach to address these barriers by leveraging the collaborative. Prudential, NJIT, and Rutgers have also supported the live local strategy by starting a fund for a renter's incentive program. This fund encourages NAC anchor employees to receive an incentive to live in select properties in downtown Newark.

RWJBH has also highlighted its anchor work with another non-traditional partner, the New Jersey Devils hockey team. *The Wall Street Journal* ran a story about the individual we contracted with to create a new urban entrepreneurial venture of making socks for our patients. But he doesn't just make patient socks; he makes socks, period. We connected him with the New Jersey Devils, who contracted with him to make three hundred thousand socks for players and for their gift shops. For a small startup, that was a huge boost, and certainly one that helped to broaden the base of the commitment in the area of local purchasing. The New Jersey Devils were already a pretty significant partner of our organization. We actually have the naming rights to their arena, known as the "RWJBarnabas Health Hockey House," and the portion of the rink we collaborate with them on is open to the community so that not just the ice hockey fans get to play on the ice, but also residents of the surrounding urban community who aren't traditionally a part of their audience in order to create opportunities for local residents to learn the game themselves. Through this partnership, we do nutrition and wellness coaching for kids. That relationship helped make them a natural partner for our anchor mission work.

When you're looking for external institutional partners, look at what they've done in the past for clues as to whether they're likely to be a good fit with the work you're doing. What seems to resonate with them? The new ownership of the New Jersey Devils is committed to making an impact in the community, so they were willing to come to the table along with our traditional partners. We seek partners that make sense because they have a heart and head for the community.

Having Trouble Finding Partners? Dig Deeper!

Just about every corporate entity puts out an annual report or puts something about their social programs on their website. If your local potential partners aren't sold on helping, find others outside of the community who are engaged in this kind of change effort and bring those companies to the attention of your local corporate community. Understand their business and their priority areas. For instance, if you know that the Federal Reserve Bank or JP Morgan Chase are committed to addressing workforce development and job training, then the partnership you're offering can be presented within that framework as a gain for them—as an opportunity. The bottom line is you need to do your homework, understand the focus of your potential partners, and find areas of intersection.

But you've got to do the research to know what's out there, in order to make a compelling case for their involvement. Being able to speak to people in a particular industry in their own language, with comprehension of what they do and what others in their industry have done, helps them understand that you're offering them something of inherent value.

Relationships are important and necessary to accomplish sustainable transformation. Nobody likes making cold calls, which is why having a background in politics, public policy, or government is so helpful for change agents. But if you just don't have an extensive policy decision maker network, you're going to have to create one. Is there someone in your orbit or your organization with that kind of background, who does have a broad network of contacts? Do your best to bring that person on board and get their help to harness those contacts.

If you're a change agent without a useful network, start building one today. It is never too late. Get on your computer and perform the research necessary to identify and model the behavior, or again, identify industry best practices by well-established, well-respected entities like the Democracy Collaborative or Anchor Institutions Task Force and the integrity-evidenced models they point to across the country. Take a look at what other hospitals and healthcare experts are doing. Take a look at what national expert and author of *The Death Gap: How Inequality Kills*, Dr. David Ansell of Rush University Medical, has been doing in Illinois. Or learn from the work of Zeev Neuwirth in his book *Reframing Healthcare* at Atrium Healthcare in Charlotte, North Carolina. Or look to ProMedica in Ohio, Common Spirit, Gunderson, and others doing impactful work. We mention these to point out the fact that this work is real and is already happening, and we need to make certain we are spreading the word. We need to let people know it's their chance to get into the water and swim too. Our communities need everyone who can help to dive in.

You are going to want to identify your fellow activists in the community; for instance, the elderly woman who gets up at every city council meeting to complain that the intersection on her street needs a traffic light instead of just a stop sign. When she stands up, everyone says, "Good evening, Mrs. Smith," so clearly everyone knows her. She gets the microphone and says, "Well, if you had just done what I asked years ago, I wouldn't have to be here now." Her tenacity and persistence make her a valued asset in the community, and she's worth knowing, because she can tell you a lot about how things have and, perhaps more importantly, have not worked there and the immediate needs of her community. You have an opportunity to vet ideas and concepts through these sacred individuals. The fact that she is so well-known for just wanting what's good for the kids who have to cross that street tells you that she's someone who's well respected in the community and is making an effort for positive change.

Don't be afraid to try. We can often spend too much time making things difficult when they're not. Everything old is new again. In a digital world of emails, texting, and social media, this work requires you to create human connection for transformative systems change. You'll be amazed how those kinds of interactions pay off, in trust and in furthering your networking efforts—and help you to create a coalition of the engaged that will support and inform your work for the community.

GUIDELINES FOR CHANGE AGENTS

- Chances are, if you've got a great idea, someone else in the community is trying to find a way to accomplish the same thing but from a different angle. How can you find these beacons? You might look in vain for stories about community-based organizations or leaders in your metropolitan/statewide daily paper, so turn to the local weekly papers, where their stories are far more likely to be featured. Certainly, your statewide newspaper will likely list folks who are doing good things in a number of communities across that state, and that's an important list to keep as well. But you also want to get closer to that community, to figure out who the people are that community tends to trust, and you will see those stories highlighted in the local weekly papers, on local cable access channels, and even on the social media sites of these locally focused platforms.

- Get out of your office and into the community. If there's an event coming up, make sure you're there and interacting with the community impact leaders. As you see these events listed, pick up the phone and call the organizers, introduce yourself, and ask to attend. It's important, and only fair, that you manage expectations. If you're coming to listen and learn, then say that; small organizations will expect that you're coming with a big check—which isn't necessarily a bad thing. But, it's important to codesign a joint effort to invest in and initiate the parameters of actual partnership.

- Talk to the head of your local clergy association, because these ecumenical servants are on the front lines and are often trusted leaders of their congregants and community. If you identify a particular faith leader as an important community pillar, attend a service at his or her house of worship. Show up—and more than once—in the church/synagogue/mosque and community before asserting a request.

- Don't be afraid to ask for help, to request introductions, to ask to sit in on meetings, to volunteer, to network, and to meet people where they are.

- Want to impress a potential partner? Do your research ahead of the meeting, not just on their organization and what it may doing, but on other, similar organizations and their efforts at supporting change in the community. Offer them a blueprint of how you can partner with them to be a solution to the issues they are trying to tackle. No one is looking for another partner who is just going to talk more about the problems; they are looking for new partners with new solutions and new resources. Show you understand, and more importantly, respect who they are and what they do. Make it easy for them to say "yes."

CHAPTER SEVEN

Socializing Your Mandate

When you're turning the ship, you need everyone pulling vigorously in the same direction. How can you as a change agent create that shared sense of mission so that those at the management level in your organization are encouraged to buy into it and to support it? Getting organizational buy-in for your project is a process and not something that can be accomplished by executive order. You can't just mandate the changing of hearts and minds; you've got to educate, inform, connect, update, and cheerlead to get your colleagues on board—from the C-suite to your frontline employees.

This work requires many willing hands to accomplish; it's going to require more of your people than simply going along to get along. If they are to become invested in the work, they have to understand the need for it and the why of it and to believe that their efforts can make a meaningful difference.

The First Step? Education

The path to success must begin with wide-ranging educational efforts, because not everyone is seeing the environment through the same lens as change agents are.

How do you help people who have lived a more comfortable, more privileged life to a better comprehension of the experience of poverty, for instance, as it's lived by those whose lives demand they constantly negotiate its challenges? It's too easy for some folks to simply dismiss poverty as an outcome of slothfulness on the part of the poor, and even now we hear people who ought to know better suggesting that if they just worked harder, for instance, the poor could rise to the working or middle class. It's not that people who think this way are heartless; they're simply misinformed, and giving them a clearer picture of the systems that have contributed to many people being born into poverty, the inevitable costs of poverty, and how those systems stymie attempts to climb out of it is key to helping them understand that the challenges go much deeper. We penalize those who are born into poverty and praise (oftentimes without reason) those who were born into wealth. As a change agent, you need to be prepared to challenge these assumptions.

How can you change hearts and minds on the topic of poverty? One of the first ways we chose was to make certain that folks were aware of how much it costs to live a poverty experience. That cost actually shows up in a variety of different ways—the amount of time it takes to get from one end of town to another when you don't have your own transportation is one measure. A commute that takes ten to fifteen minutes in a car can easily stretch into an hour or more when you've got to take two buses and a train. Now, imagine for a moment that you're trying to get across town with a sick child in order to make it to a doctor's appointment. The bus is delayed and you miss your connecting subway, so when you get to the office, you're a half hour late and you're told you missed your appointment, so your child can't be seen. You have lost a day's pay, you are out the bus and train fare you paid, your child is still sick, and there's nobody to treat him. Worse yet, you're not treated with the common decency and dignity that you're due and so you don't go further to explain what has occurred because you're in an open waiting room filled with those who appear to be the 'haves' while you and your sick and hurting child are among the 'have nots.' That's the kind of healthcare system we're trying not to be. But experiences like this are unfortunately commonplace, because the structures of healthcare systems were not created with the most vulnerable in mind.

To bring this home to our colleagues, we partnered with an organization called Think Tank, Inc., which developed an educational experiential exercise they call the Cost of Poverty Experience (COPE). What was most exciting about this was that we had been asked by our partner, the Root Cause Coalition, to help codesign what would become the healthcare version of this simulation.

Established in 2015, the Root Cause Coalition is a nonprofit, member-driven organization comprising more than sixty-five leading health systems, hospital associations, foundations, businesses, national and community nonprofits, health insurers, academic institutions, and policy centers. The coalition works to achieve health equity through cross-sector collaboration in advocacy, education, and research. The mission of Root Cause is to "reverse and end the systemic root causes of health inequities for individuals and communities through cross-sector partnerships."[12] We serve as an inaugural member of the coalition, and we have leadership representation on the advisory committee.

WHAT IS COPE?

The Cost of Poverty Experience is a 2.5-hour group learning exercise. According to Think Tank, Inc., "Through the sponsorship of the CareSource Foundation, Think Tank developed COPE with low-income individuals who shared their story to give participants an opportunity to move beyond stereotypes to a more holistic understanding of the causes and effects of poverty. Also captured in the experience is the role that the broader community plays in their interactions with low-income families." [13]

The COPE exercise was a way to help us develop the SICI practice and demonstrate to those of us who had not had the experience of living in poverty the unexpected challenges it presents. For more than a few, this point of view was both novel and revelatory—but interestingly, for some, it was very familiar indeed.

When we presented the initial COPE simulation to our internal stakeholders, there were several people who approached us afterward and said, "Listen, I need to thank you for doing this. This is how I grew up." These are successful individuals who have attained higher socioeconomic status today, who nobody would

---

12   Root Cause, accessed Sep. 6, 2019, https://www.rootcausecoalition.org/.

13   OSPHE, "2019 Health Educators Institute: Navigating Health Equity," accessed Sep. 6., 2019, https://www.ohiosophe.org/event-3451403.

have guessed had lived in poverty in their childhoods—but they understood issues like food insecurity, housing uncertainty, and racism from personal experience, and seeing the a-ha! moments taking place around them as people did the exercise felt to them like a kind of personal validation. We encouraged people to share those personal stories with their colleagues if they felt comfortable doing so, because we believe it's important that everyone understands that this isn't an us-versus-them situation. It's an us-and-we condition; it affects all of us.

SARAH LECHNER, SENIOR VICE PRESIDENT FOR POLICY DEVELOPMENT AND GOVERNMENT AFFAIRS AT RWJBARNABAS HEALTH AND CHIEF OF STAFF TO THE SOCIAL IMPACT AND COMMUNITY INVESTMENT PRACTICE

As a COPE participant, you simulate a month in the life of one of our vulnerable community members. You adopt that life and those challenges and the realities of what a day or a week or a month looks like. We had about a hundred leaders participate in the simulation from throughout our system, many on the operational and executive leadership side, but also some clinical folks.

When you begin, you're handed a card and you adopt this persona. All of these are real people and real experiences, not fabricated. Every fifteen minutes represents a week in the life of the person you're simulating. Through these experiences, you begin to see what it's like not to have a car, but to have to bring your child to school and then get to your job on time. Your employer pays you via check, so you have to go cash it at the bank but the bank closes at a certain time—will you make it? And all of this is done in a very large conference room, so you're literally walking or running from area to area throughout the conference room over a 15-minute span. It's a simple technique, but it's powerful and we got a lot of traction from it; senior executives who said, "Listen, I've always kind of dismissed our community members who don't take their medication. Like, I keep giving you these prescriptions and why aren't you filling them? Or why aren't you taking your meds? And now I'm understanding, my gosh, you're deciding between your rent, your grocery bill, or your prescription, and that's the last thing on your list."

BARRY H. OSTROWSKY, PRESIDENT AND CEO, RWJBARNABAS HEALTH

I think at least half of our people immediately embraced the idea and understood that they had to integrate it into what they did or oversaw every day. There were others who agreed intellectually that it made sense to help our communities, but really didn't know what to do about it: How could finance help? What part could materials management play? We needed to explain what it meant to incorporate this mission objective into their daily professional lives.

I told them, "Look, you're all managing very big portfolios of activity, and one of the pillars of our strategy is financial prudence and effective financial management. You already incorporate that in what you do. This will require a similar involvement and commitment, and we'll be asking for your participation and support as we put together these programs."

Another component of management had some difficulty understanding why a healthcare system would or should embrace this kind of work. The answer was that if we waited for someone else to do it—say, via government policy making—it would never get done. These folks were concerned that our organization pursuing this would consume resources that might otherwise be allocated to the things they were already doing. If this meant they couldn't recruit another great physician or weren't going to be able to develop another venue, should we be expending those resources to the potential exclusion of our more conventional strategic plans? All of them eventually came around and embraced the work.

Socialize the Mandate at the Top and Build Consensus

How do you shape things so that people at the management level in your organization are encouraged to buy into it and to support it? Then, how can you take that organizational commitment deeper than management level, to allow all employees to feel like there's a way they can contribute?

We began our efforts to socialize our mandate at the top of our corporate structure with the formation of what we call our corporate anchor roundtable, to make certain that the asset leaders over the lines that flow into making this work real had an opportunity to adapt to the change within our institution as its new mission unfolded and to adopt this work as their own.

At the table were the most senior asset leaders in every division. For human resources, that is the chief human resources officer at the corporate level; for IT, the chief information officer at the corporate level. It's the chief development officer at the corporate level and the corporate treasurer. Both the senior vice president for supply chain finance and the senior vice president for facilities and construction management were at the table too. Why these entities in particular? Not only did we want them to be early adopters of the work, we needed to ensure that we created a safe space so that these folks could ask questions about how to embed the work into daily operations and we could talk through the nuts and bolts of doing the work.

DARRELL TERRY, PRESIDENT AND CEO, NEWARK BETH ISRAEL MEDICAL CENTER AND CHILDREN'S HOSPITAL OF NEW JERSEY

Most of the resistance we heard was about pricing or concerns regarding the ability of the new vendor to be able to deliver. I don't think it was mean-spirited in any way; I think it's a legitimate concern about making sure our business operations are not negatively impacted, making sure that our margins are clean and that we're not eroding our margins and our ability to provide the high-quality healthcare we're known for. Some people who are not as in tune with our strategy will default to the lowest bidder, and that's not always aligned with what we're trying to accomplish. We're really trying to make long-term, sustainable, systemic changes, and it takes time.

A great deal of hospitals' purchasing happens in group purchasing organizations, especially in a large-scale system. We wanted to ensure we were having discussions that included our facilities and construction management, because they handle a lot of our spend, and given the size of our footprint, we have an opportunity to make real advancement in this space at a quicker pace than waiting to find supply chain opportunities as they presented themselves in new vending opportunities. For instance, we recently announced an emergency room expansion project of, at one of our hospitals, about $89 million. Initiatives like these are not small one-offs; they are large-scale projects that occur over the course of several years—and they give us an opening to create opportunity in the community. So we're designing the master plan with ample local purchasing, local hiring, utilization of small minority contractors, and living classroom internship opportunities for students in the area high school to have paid internships with architecture, engineering, and design firms in order to expose them to not just blue-collar construction jobs but the white-collar back-office jobs.

DIANA ORTIZ-CANDELEJO, DIRECTOR, ANCHOR MISSION, SOCIAL IMPACT COMMUNITY INVESTMENT PRACTICE, RWJBARNABAS HEALTH

I oversee the high level of the anchor mission initiative: hire local, buy local, and invest local. It's a work in progress, and one we're still figuring out every day. From the social impact and community investment perspective, internally, it's really been about collaborating with different asset leaders. The way we keep everyone moving in the same direction is via the corporate anchor roundtable, quarterly meetings where our CEO for the system and our EVP cochair the quarterly meeting and the different asset leaders report on the anchor mission social impact initiatives. From time to time we'll have different CEOs from different facilities on a rotational basis at these roundtables as well. I make sure we're doing this work in a very collaborative, equitable, and transparent way. I might be checking in on how many local hires to date we have and how much they earn in hourly wage and making sure it's either a living wage or that they have a pathway toward that living wage.

Recently, representatives from our pharmacy division, which had not customarily been a member of that group, came in and did a presentation on their Centers of Hope initiative that helps low-income individuals to get their medications either free or at a reduced price. Pharmacy is a very heavily regulated industry, so this was a difficult initiative to bring about. They literally had to assign a full-time team member to the project who, after a year of working through the regulatory framework, went before the pharmacy board to be questioned: How would the program be monitored? Who'd be getting assistance, and what were the criteria for choosing them? We wanted our roundtable membership to hear about this, because great ideas breed more great ideas, and hearing about them creates momentum. How did they handle the challenges attached to their initiative? Can we learn from their experience? It creates a kind of healthy sibling rivalry among them.

We also encourage these busy leaders to designate emerging leaders from their respective departments to be their social impact liaisons to the CAR, responsible for helping embed the work into daily operations in their departments and for training others. They report at the meetings, too, and it's a great opportunity for up-and-coming leaders in the organization to shine and to be exposed to a high-level leadership meeting with the CEO.

As members of the CAR, these internal leaders get to share with and hear from each other on what everyone is working on, which creates a powerful sense of forward motion and efficacy. We wanted to make it fun, too, and to remind the members of the power of their contributions to the cultural shift, to reiterate to them the mighty impact of our collective effort on a single community and upon the entire state, to essentially convey to them that they're superheroes—so naturally, we award capes and masks to them. What's a superhero without a cape?

Buy-in needs to happen at every level, because the grassroots in middle management and below is where the real momentum will start and must be sustained. And it's hard to look this work in the eye and turn away, no matter where you are in the power structure. When you realize the opportunity you as an individual and as part of a group have to effect meaningful, positive change, that's motivating. Getting people at the grassroots invested was key, because we knew their excitement about the work would bubble up to senior management and even to the facility CEO level, creating a groundswell of support.

Great internal communication is critical to this phase of the work, and the messages have to be consistent and constantly repeated: Why are we doing this? What do we mean when we say that we have changed our mission? What does this work require? What is an anchor institution? Why are we defining ourselves as one and embracing this work as part of our new mission?

SARAH LECHNER, SENIOR VICE PRESIDENT FOR POLICY DEVELOPMENT AND GOVERNMENT AFFAIRS AT RWJBARNABAS HEALTH AND CHIEF OF STAFF TO THE SOCIAL IMPACT AND COMMUNITY INVESTMENT PRACTICE

From my perspective, we have had to course correct a little bit in terms of how we do our internal communications. We've been fortunate over the last six months to have a designated communications person to help us with all of our branding, marketing, and strategy, on both the internal and external sides. That doesn't mean she does it all, but it does mean we have a central point of access, one who truly understands the work. That's helped us to realign things and provided an opportunity for us to improve on how we're doing things. I think we missed an opportunity on the internal communications side to educate folks on an ongoing basis on how we can shift our mission. At our initial launch, we did a great job presenting the "why" of the work to the board, but we're playing a little catch-up explaining the "why" to our internal communities, and I think that's where some of the challenges come in. We probably could have done more to work on that aspect, to educate as we built the plane, but we're getting better at it. In a large company, focusing on your internal audience and the "why" of the work early and often is really important.

People want and need to be informed, and not just once; they need to hear it repeatedly, read about it multiple times, and have the same solid messaging coming at them from all directions. We made videos. We issued internal communications from the top. We showed up at meetings and explained it. Our CEO effectively went on a town hall tour across our system to all of our hospitals and business offices, talking about it. Our "why" was pretty straight-forward; we continue to do work within our hospital walls and yet we're still seeing negative health outcomes in the communities where our facilities are located, and it's unacceptable. We're tired of reading about disparities and not doing anything differently in order to address them. We are changing to ensure that we are not just reading about it but taking action.

Everyone tasked with socializing the mandate needs to be singing from the same songbook, so make sure the people involved with your project are consistently on message and using the same language.

Give Everyone a Chance to Shine

Let's be honest; face time with the CEO is something most people in management would like to get a lot more of—and providing opportunities for that is something we've built into the structure of our corporate anchor roundtable. Everyone gets her or his chance to report out to the CEO on their efforts to date: their approach to the work, what challenges have met them along the road of implementa-tion, and what their outputs are at this stage, because oftentimes it's too early to have outcomes.

Language is really important, because this is a chance for us to come together and talk honestly about successes and wins along with challenges and barriers. Initially, some asset leaders were concerned that they were being brought before the CEO about work that hadn't yet borne fruit, and that felt risky to them. In an organization committed to this change, it had to be made clear that we were entitled to some failures—that we had to try things that might not work. All of the work is done under a design methodology: it's not plan, plan, plan, plan, launch, but plan, launch, review, tweak, relaunch, review, tweak. If you don't do it that way, then you are going to create an environment that is intolerant to risk, because people are naturally afraid that their failure will result in embarrassment or worse. You must foster a risk-tolerant environment or else you will stifle creativity and innovation, and in doing this work, that's the last thing you need.

> **it's not plan, plan, plan, plan, launch, but plan, launch, review, tweak, relaunch, review, tweak.**

Fortunately for us all, that isn't who our CEO is: what he wants to see is effort and intentionality. He wants to see it well thought out, but he understands this is a dynamic living laboratory, in a sense.

MICHELLENE DAVIS, EXECUTIVE VICE PRESIDENT AND CHIEF CORPORATE AFFAIRS OFFICER, RWJBARNABAS HEALTH

One individual called me before a meeting to beg off his attendance as he didn't really have anything substantive to report; I reminded him of all he'd been working on throughout the quarter and helped him to draft a list of talking points that pointed out all the forward movement he and his department had accomplished. The nature of the work means that it takes time, but progress, while iterative, is measurable.

Another part of socializing our mandate within the organization has been the creation of a group of what we call clinical ambassadors, because it's important that our clinicians understand their part in this. We've seen that many of them are strongly called to the work, especially those who work with vulnerable populations at our hospital facilities in either our urban areas, who treat a higher percentage of the elderly, or who are brave enough to share with us that they themselves come from those vulnerable populations. These people in particular lean into their work in a very real and significant way to ensure that we are providing the care to our patients, their families, and our communities in a much more comprehensive way. It's a kaleidoscopic approach that recognizes the varied needs of diverse populations and addresses them individually, rather than taking a blanket approach.

One of the doctors who serves as an ambassador is Dr. Carol Ash, the chief medical officer at one of our facilities. She is tremendously sensitive to the ALICE population—what we defined in a previous chapter as asset limited, income constrained, employed—because she's a caretaker for a family member and understands the demands that role places on those tasked with it. Once she saw herself in that role, she began to see this usually invisible population all around her. Knowing that made her eager to treat the whole person, not just the problem presenting.

The working poor who suffer from food insecurity are people we see every day; they serve our coffee, they take our breakfast orders, they smile at us when we pay a toll. They serve us as the custodians of our office buildings or assist with bringing our groceries to the car. They sit at the front desk and greet us or direct our calls with pleasantry. Are they ALICE? They may well be. And that kind of a-ha moment can happen at any level. A CEO of one of the hospitals in our system shared that he'd not been aware there was really any problem with food insecurity among the hospital employees and didn't know what we were talking about when we explained the difference between our social impact approach and traditional nonprofit community benefit efforts—until, that is, he happened to see a line of folks who were at the facility's greenhouse to use their SNAP (Supplemental Nutrition Assistance Program—formerly food stamps) benefits after our certification as the state's first hospital-based greenhouse SNAP vendor and realized that the line was full of his employees. That made a believer out of him.

That greenhouse, by the way, provides a clear example of the importance of policy leading our work. It was the first in the state to achieve certification to accept SNAP benefits, because we realized that a large percentage of the population around the hospital were dependent on that program to buy food—and that if they couldn't access the fresh produce we were providing, it wasn't going where it was most needed and we weren't being who we claimed to be. But it wasn't enough that we held this prestigious position; we also needed to work with policy makers to amend a 1940s rule that had, perhaps inadvertently, contributed to a pretty substantial inequity. You see, the provision prohibited anyone from accepting government benefit program vouchers unless their produce came from a farm of five acres or more. New Jersey is the Garden State, and this provision was originally mandated as a method of protecting the state's farmers. But it hadn't kept up with the times. As a result, it hadn't reflected the advancements of farming and as more urban growers entered the field in order to establish community gardens as an effort of beautification and food security in food deserts the prohibition kept food out of the mouths of the hungriest children. Clearly, this couldn't have been the legislative intent. The SICI policy team began working with the New Jersey Departments of Human Services and Health, who in turn had to begin working with federal agencies in order to undo this antiquated prohibition. The victory of repealing this rule ushered in automatic enrollment of hospital-affiliated greenhouses in

both SNAP and the Women, Infants, and Children (WIC) supplemental nutrition program so that the most vulnerable populations
would now have ample access to the freshest vegetables and brightest
fruit in the closest locations.

BARBARA MINTZ, SYSTEM SENIOR VICE PRESIDENT, HEALTHY LIVING AND COMMUNITY ENGAGEMENT, RWJBARNABAS HEALTH

Transforming how SNAP and WIC are delivered in New Jersey
creates real impact, not just for our neighbors here in Newark,
but throughout the state. We are particularly thrilled because
it is a critical piece in a comprehensive effort. Policy change;
the Beth greenhouse; nutrition education; our newest partnership, a satellite food pantry in partnership with the Community
Food Bank of New Jersey; and delivery of healthy food and
other essentials to pregnant women and new moms offered
by our local Shop Rite Stores will work in concert to improve
maternal and infant mortality rates, addressing many of the
social determinants. While we know black infant mortality
and black maternal mortality are the result of many factors—
one-stop shops, access to services and supports, good nutrition,
and streamlined access to benefit programs like SNAP and
WIC—these steps, combined with caring clinical care, all play a
role in increasing a woman's chance of having a healthy baby
and remaining healthy herself after delivery. This is our aim.

Are Your Fellow Workers Having Their Own Poverty Experience?

You won't know if you don't ask. We contacted the chief human resources officer and asked him to take a look at how many employees we have who are living through a poverty experience. Initially, he came back with a figure of one hundred twenty—that's a pretty small number out of a sea of an affiliated forty-four thousand—but when we furthered the discussion we realized that the federal poverty level (FPL) had been used to determine the estimated number. Well, as New Jersey is the 14th wealthiest state in the nation, the cost of living here reflects that. Hence, we pointed out that the FPL was a very different standard than that which is utilized for state benefits, because this is such an expensive state in which to live. When we asked him to run the numbers using New Jersey state benefit standards (ranging from 200% to 450% of the FPL depending on the benefits program), the number shot up—closer to approximately twenty thousand. The fact is, if you're living at the defined FPL here in New Jersey, you're probably living at the train station, because of the cost of living.

Your first response may be "let's raise their wages"—but that can backfire in ways you may not anticipate. As our CEO, Barry H. Ostrowsky, explained to a journalist when talking about the decision to raise the minimum wage, before New Jersey enacted the legislation, in our organization to $15 per hour: "As you know, there are unintended consequences, unfortunately, when you raise wages. Some households who are benefiting from their membership in public assistance programs, they no longer qualify to be in those programs. So, counterintuitively and ironically, you may pay more, but it turns out, in terms of usable funds and the ability to support lifestyles, some employees may be worse off because of that."

You don't want to run after the headline and trip over the people. That's why at every step, you must be much more thoughtful, deliberate, and methodical and, more importantly, inclusive and active in listening to the people you're trying to help.

Joining with the Community

Among the reasons so many corporate entities are not beloved by their communities is that the people who wind up working on the construction sites of their large-scale economic development projects don't look anything like the people who actually live there. When that's the case, you are sending a message to the folks who live in that community that "this is ours, not yours." But the people who live near these development projects want jobs, too; they also want to feel of value to the upkeep of their neighborhoods and their families. In addition to a few programs that shall be discussed in a moment, a part of our youth workforce development commitment includes a sizable investment in the city of Newark's Summer Youth Employment Program as well as our partnership with New Jersey Community Capital, which helps to align the city's YouthBuild program to work on our scattered site redevelopment housing project; along with opening pathways to their participation in the labor force, it's a win/win for everyone. Coupled with our partnership with Jingoli Construction and our adoption of their Competitive Edge program, we're able to take youth from the internship learning opportunity to the externship—on the construction site—opportunity.

LOURDES VALDEZ, CORPORATE DIRECTOR OF WORKFORCE DEVELOPMENT AND GRANTS, RWJBARNABAS HEALTH

Everything we do is a collaboration with outside agencies. That's why it's very important in an anchor mission of the organization to include all of the internal and external stakeholders. In order for any of these programs to be successful, we need to bring them along.

We were inspired by a local developer, Joey Jingoli, who took the initiative to create something called a Competitive Edge program. What caught our attention was that when he was doing a development project in the city of Newark, he worked with the local high schools to create something called a living classroom, in which students learn about the project and how it works . The students meet not only the people involved in the hands-on construction but also the engineers and architects. What Mr. Jingoli understood is that folks need to know what's happening in their community, and that creating pathways of understanding like this would help future workforce development.

We've helped to create apprenticeship programs in cooperation with local schools and colleges to provide opportunities for students to work on this large-scale development. Right now, our SVP for facilities and construction is Bill Cuthill, who was one of our early adopters of working in this space. We've discussed the interns he'll be bringing aboard and how the architects and engineers will include interns in their work. And while we will be paying those interns, we're looking to our private sector partners on the development project to make sure that these internships provide a useful curriculum that makes interns viable candidates for future employment; not only the blue-collar jobs, but also the white-collar, back-office jobs that access to could combat inter-generational poverty. We work, too, with local union shops to make sure that the folks who get these jobs come from the communities.

LOURDES VALDEZ, CORPORATE DIRECTOR OF WORKFORCE DEVELOPMENT AND GRANTS, RWJBARNABAS HEALTH

You have to put yourself in others' shoes in this work, to be nonjudgmental and to understand the feelings of the people you're working with—and sometimes to get creative.

For example, we had just finished an EMT program. There are two levels of exams the students have to pass; first, they have to pass the class's final exam, but there also is a national exam that they have to register for and take online to graduate. I was having some difficulty in getting them to enroll for that national registry exam, and I could see that some of them were unclear on how to do that or unsure of themselves. How could I get them all to take this necessary step? I thought to myself, "Let's have a celebration for them passing their final exam." So, I invited them to celebrate their success; I invited their families, their educators, the CHRO of the facility, and others, and we held it at the community college, where there were plenty of computers. I brought all the vouchers with me to that celebration, so they could just register for the exam right then and there, and I made sure to sit down with each of them to walk them through the process.

Our Corporate Institute for Internship is also under the social impact umbrella because what we're trying to do is to effectuate a more equitable future by looking for candidates that come from non-traditional backgrounds. It's great that a doctor wants to have his son or daughter participate in an internship program, but we're also looking to include the son or daughter of the custodian or of the food worker in the cafeteria. Where are the viable candidates from our vulnerable populations, and how can we expose them to available opportunities and recruit them into our workforce?

JOSEPH SCOTT, EXECUTIVE VICE PRESIDENT FOR HEALTH CARE TRANSFORMATION, RWJBARNABAS HEALTH

I can think of nothing better than to give somebody an opportunity; not to just give them money but give them opportunity to be able to apply and advance themselves. To me, it feels like a personal mission. One of the most gratifying experiences of my life around this work came out of a program we did. We hired local people to work in our facility as environmental service technicians—the people who clean the bathrooms and patient rooms. Then, we got a grant that allowed us to hire a teacher so those environmental service techs could then become patient care technicians. In order to become certified patient care technicians, they had to go to classes for six months after work, three hours a night, Monday through Thursday. I think we've trained over two hundred of our entry-level employees to advance to higher-paying jobs. Some of them have even gone on to become RNs.

We do a graduation for them when they finish their patient care technician course, and then we hire them for those positions, so there's not only training but also employment.

We had a husband and wife who both worked here and who

took the course together. After graduation, the husband got up and said, "When we went to class together, honestly, I think that all of us felt like we couldn't do it. But we all tried hard, we helped each other, and we all succeeded. Even more importantly, my children saw me and my wife studying at the table and took a much greater interest in their own schoolwork as a result." Now there's nothing better than that. Right?

Our mandates include local hiring, local procurement, and local investing, and we've got a number of initiatives in place to support the community. These include supporting our investment in Newark Venture Partners, an innovation hub that was started by our anchor partner Audible.com, located in Newark, to encourage urban entrepreneurship in the city of Newark. Not only are we hoping to encourage them to stay in Newark, but we have Joe Scott, our executive vice president for healthcare transformation also working with them in their infancy to help them understand what healthcare entities are looking for, so that we're helping them to create businesses that fit into the unmet needs in the healthcare IT space. And we're seeing real progress—implementing software from a local startup and procuring tools and data to assist HR in the recruitment of physicians and practical nurses from another young tech company. All firms are sponsored by Newark Venture Partner Labs and commit to conducting their business in Newark.

Hiring locally is part of every department's mandate. A recent report told us that the information technology division hired locals for ten out of the twelve positions that opened up this year. They are also committed to recruiting companies from the communities that we serve and hitting what we call the procurement sweet spot: utilizing local vendors that are minority-, woman-, veteran-, or employee-owned. That can be challenging, because many corporations who were here in the 1960s fled to the suburbs at the time of the historic Newark Rebellion. Those companies that remained tend to be smaller and midsize businesses, more often owned by minorities, women, or veterans. We're interested in shoring them up, because when others left the community they remained as a very real aspect of recreating the community.

DARRELL TERRY, PRESIDENT AND CEO, NEWARK BETH ISRAEL MEDICAL CENTER AND CHILDREN'S HOSPITAL OF NEW JERSEY

A quick story of one of the participants in the Hire Newark program: She and her husband had five boys, all of them under the age of ten. Her gaps in employment were really based around the fact that she was having babies. She had a resume that would not be attractive to most employers, yet she was smart and gifted and she completed the program with flying colors. She created her own business making cakes and became a cook for us, a chef for us, and remains employed in a hospital within the system. She and her husband bought a house as a result of this work opportunity and she just recently had her sixth baby, which is finally a girl so I think she's done!

We had partnered with Rutgers University's School of Business long before we had the systemwide affiliation agreement we have now. Rutgers and the Newark Anchor Collaborative had begun to create a database of businesses; this buy local initiative included vetting these businesses to ensure that they possessed the capacity to enter vendor opportunities with entities as large as RWJBH and other anchor members. We worked with their assistant dean of supply chain on how to build a program that would permit us more opportunity to work with diverse suppliers. How do we meet the merits of an institution that is aiming to be welcoming, open, and inclusive? What about our internal procurement processes needs to be addressed?

MICHELLENE DAVIS, EXECUTIVE VICE PRESIDENT, CHIEF CORPORATE AFFAIRS OFFICER, RWJBARNABAS HEALTH

One local business that I knew was ready to partner with us was MZM Construction. The owner of it is a woman by the name of Marjorie Perry, whom I'd known for years. She'd already built an airport and had worked on local hotels. I proposed her to our building people, who indicated they'd be willing to try her with a small project, as she had never constructed a healthcare delivery building. The first phase of it was between $30–50,000. Her response wasn't exactly overwhelming, and I had to say to her, "Marjorie, please, I'm trying to get them to be more open to this and to better understand that minority women do own companies that can get this kind of work done and done well." She signed on and worked with us for about six months. As the quality of her work became evident, they just kept adding on to the project and it eventually ballooned into a $350,000 job. They were so pleased with what she did that at the hospital's gala, they presented her with an award.

In our case, the spend is not insignificant: in 2017, for example, IT spent $10,283,856 with minority-owned firms. Our 2018 expenditures were over $11 million. In addition, for 2018, we set a target of $300,000 to 500,000 for new, local, diverse vendors and are happy to report that our total for new vendors in 2018 was more than $723,650. Utilizing our impact reports gave us a baseline, helped us to accurately monitor our progress, and held us accountable for the results.

For some, the idea of keeping our spend local was more challenging; it wasn't how things had been done, and long-term relationships existed between our managers and their vendors. But money spent on a firm in Ohio or Michigan does nothing for our local economy and misses the chance to create stimulus for our local economy. This work creates economic stimulus in the local economy. Every dollar that flows out is a dollar that could have flowed through.

How do we define local? It matters, and it can be a challenge; we're such a large corporation that it could be argued the whole state could be considered local—but the issue with that is if you go too wide in your definition, you're never really getting to the opportunity to make an impact in the vulnerable communities you're trying to help. One of the functions of the corporate anchor roundtable has been to keep that definition tight, local to our facilities first and foremost, and then, because the state simply doesn't have enough minority-, woman-, and veteran-owned businesses, to the rest of the state.

GUIDELINES FOR CHANGE AGENTS

- Your most important job in socializing your mandate is to educate your stakeholders at every level: What are you trying to accomplish? Why is it important? How will it change your institution and your community for the better? This is not a one-and-done but rather an ongoing effort. You will have to explain it many times to many different constituents. Get accustomed to it. Research reveals that most individuals need to hear a message seven times to truly absorb it.

- Ensure that everyone has a chance to shine and to contribute. That's how people begin to see themselves as part of something important and find their place in it. If that means helping people to write their reports and understand how important process is, versus just product, to progress, make that effort.

- Make sure all roads lead back to your community and your impact there.

- Create your own anchor roundtable, because it keeps people on target and communicating with each other and helps increase transparency and accountability. If your CEO or other senior leadership chairs the meetings, people are going to do their very best to look good—and are much more likely to show up!

- Celebrate your people and their victories, out loud and proudly. Make it fun.

- Define your guidelines for best practices, and make sure that all efforts are channeled through that lens.

- Use the carrot, not the stick, to motivate. Remember, these folks are being asked to take on new and additional duties beyond their original mandates. Treat them accordingly. Make it rewarding. Be respectful of their time.

- Not everyone will get on board, at least not right away. For some folks, the ideas that drive this work are very foreign. Be patient. Continue to work with them behind the scenes. Invite them to participate. Anything punitive is contrary to the spirit of the work you're trying to do. That being said, some may try to play a shell game on you. Moving items around the board does not progress the work. Be bold and brave enough to call out game playing when you see it. Aiding our communities comes with a sense of urgency.

- Bring colleagues and asset leaders with you to conferences focused on this work, so that they can see the national discussion in action, better understand how what you're doing fits into the larger scheme of things, and meet like-minded folks. It will help them understand that this isn't just your organization, but a national movement toward equity. That grows internal ambassadors who will make your case for you. The bigger the tent, the better for your work.

CHAPTER EIGHT

Mentors, Advisors, and Peers

W e've said it before, but it bears repeating: as a change agent, you're inevitably going to come up against some degree of resistance to your efforts. It's hard for some of us not to take that personally—how is it possible that any thoughtful person can't see the need for systemic reforms that address inequities and healthcare disparities?—but it's important to realize that most often, this is simply a manifestation of a natural, inherent resistance to change of any sort, especially in large-scale organizations.

The fact is that many people already feel overworked, with more than enough responsibility on their plates. They are going as fast as they can in the direction that they have always been told to go—then suddenly they're being told, "Hey, not only might there be a better way to get there, but we actually might want to go about getting there in a different manner." Change agents can tend to be idealists, enthusiastic and passionate about their cause—but not everyone is going to see it the way you do. Even if they accept the "why," the "how" can be a tougher sell, and you can find yourself becoming discouraged.

That's why it's incumbent on you to ensure you're providing yourself and your team with the mentoring and support you and they need to be successful. Here's an example: As mentioned in the previous chapter, when we first started talking about moving to local anchor procurement, most of the people involved in supply chain here knew about working with small, minority- or woman-owned businesses. But in large-scale organizations like ours, you wind up in situations where those diverse suppliers are also large multinational entities. The local piece was critical to the work we were trying to do, so we needed to provide those tasked with buying with a firm and concrete definition of what qualified as local, provide them with a list of already-vetted companies that qualified, and help them to partner with others in similar positions who had done this successfully in their own institutions across the country, to serve as sounding boards and mentors.

Where can you as a leader find mentors to help you be better at what you're trying to do? If you work for a nonprofit, chances are that at least some of the people on your board have been involved in work or have a network that supports social responsibility, social impact, and anchor institution work already. They can be tapped for advice and insights, because they've already been where you're going. They can advise you on how to deal with those natural strategic tensions and how to scale your expectations to a reasonable level.

Even the most committed will occasionally feel as though they're rolling a boulder uphill, so it's important to have a good bench of mentors, advisors, and peers; connect with who are like-minded or have been change agents in their own fields or institutions, whether those are nonprofits or for-profits. We have seen how just having an opportunity to talk with those who've experienced or are in the midst of the same kinds of frustrations that afflict us all can make it easier to keep moving forward.

Team members can and should do this for one another too. Be generous with your own mentorship and in sharing what you've learned in the process. In our case, we've been called on by partners outside of our institution to talk with other hospitals and healthcare systems considering similar work, to walk them through the difficulties they can expect to face in the early stages and to make them part of our network. It's good to know there's someone you can call when you hit roadblocks to help you work around them.

BARRY OSTROWSKY, PRESIDENT AND CEO, RWJBARNABAS HEALTH

I'm asked to speak to and mentor change efforts pretty often. I can't do all of it, but I try to pick my spots. I do it for two reasons: One, I certainly want people to know about our organization and its commitment and character, and I would like to see others endeavor in the same way, because it ultimately will help their respective communities. Two, from a very macro perspective, I do think that right now organized healthcare is in the best position to address this, at least from an intellectual and a proximity standpoint. We may not have the wherewithal and no one's really willing to reimburse us for this, but we know the clinical problems. We know the daily life challenges of members of our community, and so if we're going to sit back and wait for others to do it, I think that's kind of shame on us. And while we may not be doing it perfectly, we're situated to at least undertake it, and so I want to encourage others that are similarly situated to do so. I get to do that on those occasions when I share our thinking with others.

While I personally don't have a formal mentor, I do get together twice a year with a small group of fellow CEOs from around the country, and that opportunity to share thinking with my peers in this field is useful to me. When I first spoke to this group about social determinants, one of the CEOs I admire the most, who runs an urban hospital in Boston, said to me, "Barry, what if the social problem is potholes? Are you going to fill the potholes?" I said, "Yep. We may not do it ourselves, but we'll find people to fill them. That's exactly how we need to think, because if we're going sit with a broken traffic light for months, it's just another indication that no one's paying attention to the community."

As a mentor to others, I'm a great believer in encouraging intellectual curiosity and continuing education, particularly nowadays, when you can learn a lot about almost any subject by simply spending an hour in front of your computer. I encourage all of our management team to take advantage of the mentorship and coaching opportunities we offer, because when all is said and done, we want our folks to be as good as they can be.

Coaches and Advisors

When you're connecting people to mentors, advisors, and support systems, don't forget about the strengths that coaches can bring to the table. A good coach will listen and provide insights, support, and advice. Every star athlete has a coach; most star executives do have or have had coaches too. As a leader, providing your stars with coaching can help them reach the next level of performance, and getting a coach of your own gives you someone who's an expert on performance but blessedly disinterested in the specifics of your work, so that you can speak freely about obstacles and opportunities, air your frustrations, and be honest about your concerns that you'll never meet your own goals. Having that person there to help you navigate through it all, offering advice on working with others of varied backgrounds and experience, can be a real lifeline when your common sense is telling you, "This is never going to get off the ground."

Advisors, too, have a role to play; someone with a strong background and experience in the kinds of work you're trying to do can steer you around pitfalls and offer useful strategic advice. Karen Proctor, CEO of Harbour Workshops, is a brilliant beacon of hopeful light whose compassionate advisement is matched only by her deep knowledge of social innovation and extensive experience in corporate social responsibility. Karen possesses a superpower of utter hope and belief in our team's ability to conquer the world. She is, without question, one of the most prolific thinkers in this space on the planet and has served as an advisor to many in the SICI practice. These support systems will aid you in building the resiliency this work demands and the nimbleness to go over, under, sideways, or around the difficulties you're inevitably going to face. Whether you find these kinds of mentors in leadership groups or by taking the initiative to get in touch with others who are further along and more experienced than you are, seek them out. People want to help and know mentorship isn't a one-way road. The people to whom you're likely to be drawn will be drawn to you as well. Let's underscore the earlier-stated adage, "Success has many fathers, but failure is an orphan." The fact is that when like-minded people see you advancing and making progress in the work, they're going to be inclined to want to help you get where you're going. Mentors may even approach you to begin a relationship and share their wisdom and experience.

Look Beyond the Silo

When you're looking for a mentor, be willing to look outside of your own specific area or silo. People whose experience doesn't exactly match your own can give you valuable, fresh perspectives that will help you look at your work through fresh eyes. And honestly, all leaders face certain common challenges when they're trying to turn the ship, regardless of what kind of a ship they're piloting. Consider, too, taking on a spiritual, values-based mentor, someone who will help you more clearly define your core values and stick to them. That can really be helpful when you find yourself at a crossroads.

Most of all, you want to connect with people who can help you to see things through a broader lens. They help to provide you with the bird's-eye view of every situation. They help you to plan better for the long term, because they've been there before, and they can tell you what's around the bend: "Yes, I've been in a similar situation, and this is where we came out on the other end" is a valuable point of view. Life goes on even as we do our work, and mentors can also provide that listening ear and caring voice when your personal life throws you a painful curve. One of the best things that we've done here is to introduce a formal mentorship program in our Women's Leadership Alliance, to broaden the base of mentors and create opportunities for mentees.

As your efforts progress and people hear about what you're doing, you will find yourself being approached to serve as a mentor to others. Even if that just means helping that person to connect with someone they have been waiting to meet that you may already have some relationship with, make the effort. But when you feel a sense of connection and alignment, don't be afraid to say yes—and don't hesitate to hold their feet to the fire; there's nothing wrong with giving mentees a little homework to do or telling them honestly when they're wasting your time by being underprepared or not specific enough about their needs and questions. If you share values and care about the same kinds of things, it makes the relationship that much more likely to be fruitful for both of you. As a change agent, you're likely to be a lifelong learner, and there's an element of self-evolution when you begin to use your experience to aid others.

When you're considering mentoring someone, it's important to get clear at the outset of the relationship on just what the other person's expectations are and how they match up with yours; ask questions like, "What are your expectations in this mentorship relationship, what are you looking to get out of this, and how? What do you believe you need from a mentor most, and how best do you believe that you receive it?" A lot of folks think they want a mentor, but sometimes what they really want is a private cheerleader they can count on to reaffirm how great they are. That's not what the relationship should be. Your mentor has to be able and willing to offer constructive criticism, and you as a mentee need to be willing to listen. Real leaders are going to seek out these kinds of honest relationships, because real leaders want to get better, grow, and change in ways that will stretch and push them to attain impact.

Use Reviews as a Mentoring Opportunity

As a leader, part of your job is likely to give your team performance evaluations. These shouldn't be strictly top-down, but rather two-way conversations. How does that individual learn best? How can you adjust your leadership style to help them succeed? Do they want greater responsiveness? More feedback? More responsibility? What vision do they have for their career? Are there stretch assignments they can take to help build the requisite skills to become an ideal candidate for that next promotional opportunity? And even while being honest about what you see as their performance shortfalls, make sure they know that they are valued, their contribution is significant, you're looking for ways to support their efforts, and you want to help them get what they need in order to be more successful—that you're there to work with them to make success happen.

Look for mentorship for your whole effort too, along with more personal mentorships and advisors. We communicate as an institution with other institutions and groups of institutions who are doing this work, because they help us to think more broadly in the space and to avoid costly errors as we expand. The cohort of experts these kinds of relationships will create for your institution will bring you to a higher level of effectiveness more quickly. In our organization's case, it's helped us hold ourselves to higher standards. SICI has formed an external advisory council made up of individuals from a variety of backgrounds nationwide to help us keep a broad view of our work. It's so easy to become insular and myopic if you're only talking to each other. Even if you agree to concentrate your efforts in a specific and narrowly focused way, it's important to make certain you're doing that in a way that identifies the broadest areas of opportunity within your purview.

Mentorship can also be a part of your corporate mission, as it has become a part of ours in making sure that young people within the organization and in the community reap opportunities for education and experience provided by those who contract with us to build or provide services. It's a win/win for all concerned.

DARRELL TERRY, PRESIDENT AND CEO, NEWARK BETH ISRAEL MEDICAL CENTER AND CHILDREN'S HOSPITAL OF NEW JERSEY

As part of our $100 million construction project, we have engaged a signage company so that we could evaluate our current signage and create a more comprehensive approach to wayfinding and signage. When we were making the decision about which company we were going to select, I interjected and told them that whomever we select needs to take a couple of students from one of the high schools here and introduce them to the signage world. When I was growing up and in high school, I didn't know that signage was a profession. You don't often think of it as being a lucrative business, one that could be very rewarding and pays well. Now they have incorporated a couple of students from local high schools who will participate with the whole signage plan from the very beginning to completion. They will learn skills that would not normally be available to them.

We are also including students in the construction project. Everybody that we're dealing with, everybody that we're paying money to for big projects and the like, we're trying to figure out how we can make our community benefit from it.

GUIDELINES FOR CHANGE AGENTS

- Enlist the support you need both personally and institutionally early on. Reach out, network, talk to your boss, and join others who are similarly inspired and get their advice.

- Invest in a coach; interview several professionals before you choose your coach. Seek out someone who has similar values and who understands the difficulties in creating a new initiative or facing a similar professional and personal challenge. Ideally, that will be a person who has been a change agent themselves or was in an organization that greatly changed; perhaps someone who guided an organization through a merger and acquisition or even a bankruptcy. You can't learn how to be resilient from a person who's never had to develop their own resiliency or been tested by life.

- Look, too, for people who were at a level similar to or higher than yours in their respective organizations, because those people understand the pressures involved.

- Don't neglect your responsibility to mentor others. Watching your mentee have a breakthrough, seeing them climb and evolve to become the best they can be, personally and professionally, is incredibly gratifying.

CONCLUSION
Into the Future

As this book goes to press, the ship is turning slowly but inexorably as the understanding of and support for the organization's new mission and goals grows. Increasingly, every choice made—whether that's in hiring, purchasing, or contracting—is being examined through the lens of our mission, and it's great to see the results taking shape.

BARRY OSTROWSKY, PRESIDENT AND CEO, RWJBARNABAS HEALTH

This work takes a lot of perseverance, both in and outside the organization. It takes a level of humility to understand what you're trying to accomplish, and of course a lot of cultural competence. If you come to this expecting quick success, or if you get depressed that you've only improved three lives in the last six months, then this isn't for you, because it's going to be like that. At some point, there will be greater scale to the improvement of lives, but it takes a while to get there. It's very difficult to declare victory in this: progress you'll be able to highlight, either rapidly or on a regular basis, but ultimate success will take a while.

I think this is something that evolves on a continuous and regular basis, but I'm delighted by how it's been embraced by people in the organization and by the visibility it's gotten with folks outside the organization, even nationally, as we proceed. We share whatever we do with anyone who's interested, and we learn from others who have done great things.

We continue to learn and tweak our approach on how we do business in the community. Yes, we're actively seeking opportunities to do business with smaller local companies run by women, minorities, and veterans. But we're also ensuring that there's a different pathway for payment to them, because a small business or a startup can't necessarily wait ninety days for payment, as is common with big, established companies, so we have shortened the time between invoicing and payment to accommodate them. Dignity for our business partners is part of the deal.

We continue to build partnerships with corporations in our areas; for instance, as mentioned, we have an investment in the Newark Venture Partners Labs, which is an IT incubator the Audible company has set up. As these startups find their feet and thrive, we expect to see community wealth building at a quick pace. We're hoping to see similar incubators across the state, aimed at making it possible for those who have experienced the disparate impact of systems of exclusion to build their capacity and their knowledge space and to grow, but also to be prime sources for contracting opportunities.

We strive to do the kind of work that helps to build up and give chances to those within these communities, but in more than just a one-off, arbitrary, low-hanging-fruit kind of way. How can we continue to rework our system so that these businesses are an inherent part of it, and are benefited as a result as well? As an example, it's not just a matter of choosing to use a local caterer for a special event; it's how we can partner them with our food service vendor to make them a part of a long-term, sustainable revenue line.

Hopefully, that's what the future will look like; equity will just be the way things are. It won't require anyone to rework a contract, create a rider, or have a special meeting. It will simply be the way we do business, as a natural outgrowth of our fully embracing the new mission of the institution. Everyone will get it; not just everyone in the C-suite, but also every maintenance worker, security person, and nurse will understand why we are doing this and how all of it helps to lead us to a place where our communities are healthier. It will become second nature and a part of our ongoing culture.

We would like to see the community thrive around us and see more of those who work here decide to live here too. Doctors who work here and currently live in the suburbs would choose to open offices here. We want to work more closely with the community—to help educate first-time parents on what to expect and what to do, for instance. Ideally, we'd like to make our mission redundant—that the community is so healthy, well-fed, and well-employed that our efforts to improve it are no longer necessary—but we realize that's not a realistic picture. We know that folks will always need care. Even so, that's the equitable ideal we work toward, and it continues to be a work in progress.

That's why the mission has to continue to evolve and change. Every day we need to look and ask ourselves: what new, innovative thing can we do to ensure we have partnered with our community in a way that keeps them engaged and excited about their care, that makes it easy, accessible, and affordable? How can we support community health and provide healthcare with the same ease of use and convenience that Amazon sells its goods or Google and Facebook entice their users to engage? What concerted effort are we making in healthcare to ensure that we are engaging with folks in the way they want us to, and what are we learning and how are we moving to make that engagement easier? Are there kiosks offering food sustainability options or urban agriculture hubs accepting government benefit vouchers as a result? What are we doing to ensure that we are literally changing the game?

Our hope going forward is that at every level of our hospitals, the people in them look more like our communities; the thought leaders, the board members, and the front line. As we interface with our consumers, we want them to see themselves and know they're welcome here, cared for here, and treated equitably.

Are we ever going to say, "Okay, we've done enough vending with our local businesses?" No—because our survival should be linked to theirs, and theirs can be enhanced by ours. We need to be that much more diligent about ensuring that everyone else around us is doing well too. This is not either/or; this is yes/and work. We would love to see all GPOs begin to adopt this mission-centric attitude and these methodologies so that they're identifying the local businesses and working with them to help them expand.

Can this work be expanded to our recruitment across the clinical space? As we talk about hiring locally and wanting to ensure there's diverse spend, it'd be great if we had that same kind of dialogue as we look at clinician recruitment. How are we investing with partners to ensure that we are encouraging future generations of clinicians from diverse backgrounds? What are we doing to encourage those who come from the community to return to the community when they're done with their studies, to practice and live? Can we work with medical schools to be sure these students are connected to efforts like ours, so that they feel a part of it, and can see a future for themselves both within their clinical specialties and in the management hierarchy? The evidence reveals that healthcare disparities may be reduced more expediently with the addition of more clinicians of color. How can we act to change the paradigm to make that happen?

The quest is for equity; we're not looking to push people away from the table, but rather to build a bigger table with more chairs and invite those who previously haven't had the opportunity due to systemic and structural historical disenfranchisement to join us and our efforts.

Find Ways to Let Others Share the Spotlight

When your efforts are earning you attention and showing signs of progress and success, you'll be busier than ever, because every success ideally will beget more and more expansive efforts. It's also very likely that like-minded people in your space who want to begin their own work will call on you for help and input. You'll be invited to address conferences and conventions, sit on boards, advise, and mentor. These are all great things, and certainly you want to encourage others. But be wary of spreading yourself too thin, because the temptation will be to say yes more often than you should. Use these invitations when they come as a way to encourage more of your colleagues to enter the space. Most importantly, do not be deceived into believing that talking about the work is the same as doing the work. It is not. Be dedicated first to doing the work. Your work is life-saving work but only so long as you are continuously doing it!

MICHELLENE DAVIS, EXECUTIVE VICE PRESIDENT AND CHIEF CORPORATE AFFAIRS OFFICER, RWJBARNABAS HEALTH

RWJBH SICI also covers our volunteer employee engagement efforts. Since my role within the organization is mainly focused on our external stakeholders, what I have found is that often the requests that come to me for community-based organization board membership might be better directed to someone with more knowledge about a specific area of interest; for instance, a nonprofit dedicated to abuse victims attempting to recruit me really needed an auditor. I was able to connect them with the system's chief auditor, who was a much better fit. He's a great guy, stepped up to volunteer to serve on their board, and has been working with them for the last several years, with the support and help of his entire team. This experience has also informed his view of the community in a powerful way, and he's helped us all to understand and support this community need even better.

When the business and industry association came to ask my CEO to be on their board, he passed their request along to me; I was able to provide diversity of thought and background by nominating one of the two women who are presidents of hospitals in the system. Deanna Sperling, president and CEO of our behavioral health hospital, joined the board. She brings a behavioral health perspective and the association has benefited tremendously.

We have a relationship through the practice with Cristo del Rey Schools and their Christ the King School in Newark; we pay the school via a corporate donation that helps pay tuition, and they send us four high school students from underresourced backgrounds to do an externship throughout the year. All the students who go to this particular high school graduate and go on to college, but more than that, they traditionally get tremendous amounts in scholarships. The externship gives them an inside view of our operations. The school asked me to be on their board, because they knew I shared a similar background with their students, most of whom come from very challenging backgrounds. Dr. Mary Ellen Clyne, president and CEO of Clara Maass Medical Center, grew up in the foster care system and knows the struggle, yet went on to receive her bachelor's in nursing, as well as her master's and then later her PhD. She's the CEO of this hospital. She's a great example to the students and a wonderful ambassador for the work, as are all the people who volunteer from our organization in the community.

I would encourage change agents to make certain you are being strategic in widening your tent and choose your ambassadors with care. There are times when folks can be bulls in china shops. I've had to do some cleanup work when these kinds of relationships haven't worked for one reason or another. Be judicious and protective of the community and the community members who have decided you're worthy of their trust. Really be protective of those relationships so they are not harmed. Once those relationships are fractured, they're tough to mend.

Remember, it takes a team to get this work done. We're still at the baby steps phase, but every bit of progress has impact. Even the way in which we pay our employees has changed, thanks to some thoughtful work by our treasurer, Eileen Urban, because our employees are our first community. Are there persons among our employees living in areas that lack bank branches? Are they practicing the traditional trend of these areas to use check cashing stores that charge high fees or have predatory payday loans? Let's change things so they're paid via a debit card and not penalized for not having a checking account when they live in an area that does not have a bank. Are they saving for retirement? Many were not, but now thanks to her and others, plans are being put in place to help and encourage them to do so. As written about so eloquently in Angela Glover Blackwell's "The Curb Effect," when you begin to focus on the most vulnerable, those who are at the bottom of that pay scale, when you change systems in order to accommodate them, you're actually helping everyone above them on that pay scale.

And the work touches everyone—so often in ways you won't have anticipated. One of our vice presidents stopped one of us in the hall the other day to say, "I grew up on food stamps, and so I really appreciate the way in which you have us focused on those members of the population. This is fantastic." Then there are those who have been part of our employee engagement and skills-based volunteering and reported back, "We went there for our employee engagement week of service. I realized how close it is to my home, and so my family has been volunteering ever since."

The truth is, even the most traditional hierarchical organization can become an agent for change—even if it's not in its DNA.

GUIDELINES FOR CHANGE AGENTS

- Once you find and start working with the like-minded people in your institution, make sure you're all supporting each other. It's important to ensure that everyone is rowing in the same direction. Often, once people become energized, they want to act; think of ways in which to engage early adopters in order to capture their energy and direct their involvement.

- Lean on friends outside of the institution who understand the challenges and issues you're facing, and don't be afraid to ask for their input or expertise—especially as you're just starting up and may not yet have the staff or support you need within the institution. When you're feeling bleak about the prospects of success, those friends will remind you that you, in fact, were made for this. They will pull out your faith files and remind you of the last time you went through that really terrible, no good, very bad day, when it seemed like you were surrounded by nothing but walls, and you found the strength to jump over them.

- Have faith in something greater than yourself, because you'll need it and exercise it. Whether that's by going to your house of worship, prayer, meditation, chanting—whatever it is you use to center and feed your spiritual core—when everything is swirling around you, it will help to keep you from being knocked out of your center.

- Keep going. The distractions are meant to derail you. Keep going. As tough as it may be to change something, it can be done. Impossible is an illusion. And remember—diamonds and pearls are formed under pressure. As hard as that pressure can be to take, the end result is a thing of beauty—and our communities deserve to be beautiful things.

Appendix

Changing Missions, Changing Lives describes how RWJBarnabas Health moved to addressing the clinical and the social factors that affect health. The book details our efforts to gain buy-in, build internal and external resources, and create a movement across a large healthcare system. While much of the discussion focused on our prototype city—Newark, New Jersey—similar processes have occurred in each of our RWJBH facilities. Following are a few tools and links that have been critical as we embarked on this journey. We hope that they can help you as you move forward to create change.

Identify Your Needs

We indicated the importance of always assessing the need. This is critical to gain and maintain buy-in. Never assume that everyone comes with the same knowledge about the needs of communities. When describing needs, it is critical to provide both quantitative data (the numbers, facts, and figures) as well as quantitative data (the stories and testimonials). Because each of our hospitals is located in a unique community with its own challenges and opportunities, we began with an analysis of each facility's Community Health Needs Assessment (CHNA). To view the CHNA data from each of the RWJBH facilities, visit: https://www.rwjbh.org/why-rwjbarn-abas-health-/community-health-needs-assessment/. CHNA data is important because it involves the community and community-based providers.

In addition to CHNA data, we continually look to national and state data, including but not limited to:

- World Health Organization: https://www.who.int/data/gho

- US Census American Factfinder: https://factfinder.census. gov/faces/nav/jsf/pages/index.xhtml

- Data from state departments such as Health, Human Services, Education, Labor, etc.

- United Way ALICE Research Center: https://www.united-foralice.org/national-comparison

- County Health Rankings and Roadmaps: https://www.countyhealthrankings.org/

Focus Your Efforts

As stated in the text, RWJBH knew that it could not "boil the ocean," so the organization needed to identify key pillars and priority areas on which to focus. We also needed a concise way to ensure that others understood our work. To this end, the newly formed Social Impact and Community Investment practice created a vision and a mission to ensure that all understood the charge. In addition, the practice developed the following model to describe our work.

Vision: All New Jerseyans live in—and contribute to—socially connected and economically thriving resilient communities.

Mission: Improve health for all New Jerseyans by strategically working to foster health promoting environments and conditions across the key social determinants of health. Our work contributes to healthy people, healthy homes, and healthy communities.

The model is effective because it provides the concise mission, right in the center. It illustrates our commitment to buy, hire, and invest local, which is central to RWJBH meeting its mission, as we understand the criticality of building and sustaining local economies. The model then illustrates the five pillars that are further defined by priority interventions. Surrounding the whole of the work is policy, systems change, and equity, which we know will exponentially increase the impact of our work. Finally, the model depicts an iterative and dynamic environment by stating our constant commitment to evaluate, learn, and redeploy, as required.

Once the SICI team identified areas of focus, it further defined its work through the creation of a strategic plan. The strategic plan identified objectives and tactics to meet the goals for each pillar. To view a copy of the 2019-2020 SICI Strategic Plan Summary, visit: http://magazine.barnabashealth.org/rwjbh-social-impact-report-2019-2020/html5forpc.html?page=0.

Measure Your Progress

This remains a work in progress, but we know that because this work is different and new, compared to the traditional efforts of a health-care system, it is essential to track, report, and measure progress. We do this in a variety of ways. First, our internal corporate asset leaders complete an impact report, as described in the book, at the Corporate Anchor Roundtable to demonstrate to the CEO and their colleagues the work that their departments are doing to meet the new mission.

In addition, we have developed quarterly reporting forms for our facility leads and our community-based partners, which become a piece of the evaluation tool used by the corporate SICI team to report progress toward meeting objectives, tactics, outputs, and outcomes. The tools encourage the reporting of both quantitative and qualitative data, and they require internal and external partners to report on shared metrics, while maintaining the integrity of their unique programs. Following are a few examples of the tools we have developed.

IMPACT REPORT

The purpose of this report is to surface key information and indicators to inform the SICI project/program management team so that we can drive quality performance and accountability across the RWJBH system. This is a project/program's primary reporting mechanism. Attach any indicators/tracking reports as an Addendum.

Asset Leader and/or Departmental Social Impact Liaison:

Impact Area:

PROJECT SUMMARY
Briefly summarize work

MILESTONES AND ACCOMPLISHMENTS
Bullet key milestones and accomplishments since last report

PROJECT PROGRESS
Briefly describe overall progress

PROJECT ISSUES & LESSONS LEARNED
Indicate issues and lessons learned

PROJECT RISKS & NEXT STEPS
Indicate risks that may impede completion of the project, how you intend to overcome and specific next steps

QUARTERLY REPORTING FORM

In an effort to improve health, social, and economic outcomes; promote health equity; and eliminate healthcare disparities, RWJBarnabas Health's Social Impact and Community Investment (SICI) Practice seeks to:

- Address the social needs of the region's residents

- Invest in the communities in which RWJBH maintains anchor institutions

- Promote strategic systems change that results in sustainable outcomes for all New Jerseyans

While meeting the RWJBH mission to improve the health of New Jersey by addressing the clinical and social factors that affect health is the responsibility of each RWJBH employee, the SICI team tracks progress towards meeting the System's imprint on the individuals and communities we serve. This form is designed to record and track all of the social impact and community investment activities in which your facility is involved.

FACILITY:

PERSON REPORTING:

SECTION 1: ECONOMIC STABILITY (CHECK ALL THAT APPLY)

☐ FOOD SECURITY: Strengthen local supply chain; facilitate efficient food distribution models; advocate for policies that support community farming, access to food support programs, and expand access to healthy, affordable foods in communities.

☐ YOUTH WORKFORCE DEVELOPMENT: Facilitate training and internship programs for youth; increase access to internship and workforce development programs for students in targeted communities.

☐ ACCESS TO SOCIAL SERVICES AND SUPPORTS: Implement SDOH screening; develop standard protocols to connect individuals to social supports.

Briefly describe your **ECONOMIC STABILITY** project(s):

_____

_____

Have there been any substantive changes to your **ECONOMIC STABILITY** project(s) since last quarter?

☐ Yes

☐ No

If yes, please describe:

_____

ECONOMIC STABILITY OUTPUTS/OUTCOMES

	Q1	Q2	Q3	Q4	CUM
Number of local farmers engaged in efforts at your facility					0

List the unique small, local, minority, women, or veteran owned businesses you contracted with in your economic stability projects (include total spend with each vendor. Please list below. Attach additional sheets as needed.

Name	Total Spending
TOTAL	$0.00

Number of local hires as a result of economic stability projects. Please include zip code of residence. Attach additional sheets as needed.

Targeted Zip Code	Hires by Quarter				
	Q1	Q2	Q3	Q4	CUM
					0
					0
TOTAL	0	0	0	0	0

Number of individuals educated via the WOW mobile unit at your facility or a location in your community in concert with your SICI team. Please list dates and venues:

Date	Location	Individuals Educated by Qtr.				
		Q1	Q2	Q3	Q4	CUM
						0
						0
						0
	TOTAL	0	0	0	0	0
Number of individuals who participated in cooking demonstrations and learned to prepare healthy local produce						
Number of patients that you referred to state and federal food support services						
As a result of your referrals, number of patients that got connected to SNAP						
As a result of your referrals, number of patients that got connected to WIC						

Number of students involved in workforce development efforts tracked by zip code					
Number of students involved in facility workforce develop-ment efforts who are hired by the facility following graduation					
Number of students involved in facility workforce develop-ment efforts who are hired by a local partner or organi-zation following graduation					
Number of students involved in facility workforce develop-ment efforts who go to college following graduation					
Number of students involved in facility workforce develop-ment efforts who go to the armed forces following graduation					
Months following housing					

Number of patients screened for the SDOH (please attach the tool you are using and describe above in the description the population you are screening)					
Number of unique individuals that have been educated about violence prevention					
Of those, how many were clinicians?					
Community leaders?					
Educators?					
Number of first responders who use MyStrength					
Number of first responders who engage in the Health Challenge					
Number of patients seen by Trauma Navigator					
Recidivism rate of participating patients					

Number of unique small, local, minority, women, or veteran owned businesses you contracted with in your neighborhood and built environment projects (include total spend with each vendor). Please list below. Attach additional sheets as needed.

Name	Total Spending
TOTAL	$0.00

Number of local hires as a result of neighborhood and built environment projects **(i.e., Community Health Workers from neighborhood hired or any other staff hired as a result of the grant** or SICI project). Please include zip code of residence. Attach additional sheets as needed.

Targeted Zip Code	Hires by Quarter				
					0
					0
					0
TOTAL	0	0	0	0	0
Facility Specific Outputs/Outcomes					

Testimonials/Stories: Please provide stories, quotes, and append photos that better describe your work in this area.

Additional Information: Please provide any additional information about any of your projects that was not covered above. Challenges, opportunities, etc.

Tell Your Story

The SICI team collaborated with both its internal communications and marketing team, as well as external partners and consultants to convey its new focus on social issues. Through speaking engagements, print, and digital media, RWJBH continually seeks to elevate the issues and provide potential solutions.

To find out more about the Social Impact and Community Investment Practice at RWJBH, to get updates, and to see our work in action, visit: https://www.rwjbh.org/why-rwjbarnabas-health-/social-impact/.

About the Authors

BARRY H. OSTROWSKY, PRESIDENT AND CHIEF EXECUTIVE OFFICER, RWJBARNABAS HEALTH

Barry H. Ostrowsky is the president and chief executive officer of RWJBarnabas Health, New Jersey's largest, most comprehensive integrated healthcare delivery system, with a service area that includes more than five million residents. He is spearheading a systemwide endeavor to promote healthier living for employees and community members and develop an effective strategy to address the true social needs of our diverse communities.

RWJBarnabas Health includes eleven acute care hospitals (five are teaching hospitals), three children's hospitals, a pediatric rehabilitation hospital, ambulatory care centers, geriatric centers, a freestanding behavioral health center, New Jersey's largest statewide behavioral health network, comprehensive home care and hospice programs, pharmacy services, multisite imaging centers, an accountable care organization, and medical groups with primary and specialty care physician practices. The system is comprised of thirty-three thousand employees (making it the second-largest private employer in New Jersey), nearly nine thousand physicians (representing more than 40 percent of the state's actively practicing physicians), and one thousand residents and interns.

Mr. Ostrowsky joined Saint Barnabas Medical Center in 1991 as executive vice president and general counsel and served in the same role when Barnabas Health was created in 1996. At Barnabas Health, he became president and chief operating officer in 2010 and president and chief executive officer in 2012. In April 2016, with the merger of Barnabas Health and Robert Wood Johnson Health System, he assumed his present position. Mr. Ostrowsky was previously a senior partner at Brach, Eichler.

Among active memberships, he serves on the boards of the New Jersey Chamber of Commerce, Public Media NJ, Inc. (operator of NJTV), and the New Jersey Performing Arts Center. He is a member of the American Hospital Association Health Care Systems Governing Council.

In 2016, NJBIZ named Mr. Ostrowsky the Executive of the Year in Business in New Jersey, and he has repeatedly been named to the NJBIZ Health Care Power 50 list of the most powerful people in New Jersey healthcare and to the Power 100 list, which includes the state's most influential people in business. He has also been named by Becker's Hospital Review as one of "300 Hospital & Health System Leaders to Know."

Mr. Ostrowsky received a BA from Rutgers University and a juris doctorate from the University of Tennessee School of Law.

MICHELLENE DAVIS, ESQ., EXECUTIVE VICE PRESIDENT AND CHIEF CORPORATE AFFAIRS OFFICER

With a career built on excellence and punctuated by firsts, Michellene Davis has been named one of the most influential and powerful leaders in healthcare by entities such as Modern Healthcare, Becker's Hospital Review, and NJBIZ, among others. In her current role as executive vice president and chief corporate affairs officer of RWJBarnabas Health, Ms. Davis is the first woman and first person of color to ascend to the position of executive vice president in its history. Michellene Davis oversees the following departments: social impact and community investment, policy development and governmental affairs, healthy living and community engagement, and global health.

The RWJBarnabas Health Social Impact and Community Investment Practice leverages the system's range of assets to advance a culture of health and lift the quality of life in New Jersey communities. With a programmatic emphasis on ensuring health equity, the practice spearheads innovative social impact and external affairs initiatives that address the social, economic, and environmental conditions that have a significant impact on health outcomes. The policy arm leads the practice as it seeks to change systems, structures, and policies to create a more equitable future for all New Jerseyans.

Before joining RWJBarnabas Health in 2009, Ms. Davis proudly served the state of New Jersey in several inaugural roles, including as the first African American chief policy counsel and the first African American acting NJ state treasurer responsible for a state budget of over $30 billion, where she founded the NJ Department of the Treasury's Office of Supplier Diversity and Division of Minority and Women Owned Businesses. She was the youngest executive director of the New Jersey Lottery in state history.

Active in a diverse array of civic organizations, Michellene began her legal career as a trial litigator, is an honors graduate of Seton Hall University, and holds a juris doctorate from Seton Hall School of Law. She also received an executive education certificate in corporate social responsibility from the Harvard Business School and a Wharton executive education certificate in social impact strategy.

Acknowledgments

The Social Impact and Community Investment (SICI) Practice at RWJBarnabas Health prides itself on collaboration. Every day we have the privilege to codesign with smart, committed change makers who transform lives and the communities in which they live.

We must first thank and applaud our internal champions. Change is hard. From our asset leaders to our SICI facility leads to those who have readily "volunteered" to serve as change agents (you know who you are!), you have embraced our shift from healthcare to health, ensuring that every day we are helping to build healthier communities. You have been innovative and daring and challenged yourself and our organization to think in new and creative ways. This work could not and cannot be done without you—for this we thank you and appreciate you.

Next, we *must* salute our state and local partners, the vast network of traditional and nontraditional partners that are catalysts in this work. Our partners work across a broad set of issues and sectors. They include small nonprofit organizations and huge academic institutions; they are houses of worship and advocacy organizations interested in the infrastructure of our communities. Our partners are policy makers, farmers, doctors, law enforcement officers, teachers, social workers, students, and moms. Each and every partner, each and every voice, matters. Thank you for all you do to create impact in your communities and a healthier New Jersey.

Finally, we could not do it without our partners on the national and global levels. This includes our fellow healthcare organizations, policy thought leaders, national nonprofit organizations, and policy makers. It is through your hard work that we understand we are not alone in this struggle. Thank you for your continued insight and thought leadership.